DALE CARNEGIE'S

Scrapbook

A TREASURY

OF THE

WISDOM OF THE AGES

www.snowballpublishing.com

info@snowballpublishing.com

For information regarding special discounts for bulk purchases, please contact
Snowball Publishing at

sales@snowballpublishing.com

1

Self-confidence was always at the top of the list of qualities Dale Carnegie tried to instill. In his public speaking courses, attaining confidence was the step that broke the barrier to all other goals. We can give ourselves confidence by being enthusiastic—and showing it. Courage rests on self-confidence, as does the ability to profit from adversity. ﾂ

WINSTON CHURCHILL

ONE OUGHT never to turn one's back on a threatened danger and try to run away from it. If you do that, you will double the danger. But if you meet it promptly and without flinching, you will reduce the danger by half. Never run away from anything. Never!

DWIGHT D. EISENHOWER

HAVE YOU actually measured up? If you don't have that courage to look at yourself and say, Well, I failed miserably there, I hurt someone's feelings needlessly, I lost my temper—which you must never do except deliberately—you don't measure up to your own standards.

ELEANOR ROOSEVELT

NO ONE can make you feel inferior without your consent.

CARDINAL JAMES GIBBONS

I HAVE lived eighty-six years. I have watched men climb up to success, hundreds of them, and of all the elements that are important for success, the most important is faith. No great thing comes to any man unless he has courage.

——————————❖⟨❖⟨:❖⟨C⟩❖⟩❖⟩❖——————————

from the writings of DALE CARNEGIE

WOULD YOU LIKE to have more courage? Here are five short rules, which, if you will follow them, I guarantee will increase your store of fortitude.

1. Act as if you were courageous. This makes you a bit braver as if one side of yourself had been challenged and wished to show it was not wholly afraid.

2. Pause to reflect that others have had to face great discouragements and great obstacles and have overcome them. And what others have done, surely you can do.

3. Remember that your life forces move in a sort of rhythm and that if you feel depressed and without the power to face life you may be at the bottom of the trough; if you will keep up your courage, you will probably swing out of it by the very forces which at the moment are sucking you down.

4. Remember you feel more defeated and downcast at night than during the daylight hours. Courage comes with the sun.

5. Courage is the measure of a big soul. Try to measure up.

————————————————————————————————

CHARLES F. KETTERING

I HAVE found that if I have faith in myself and in the idea I am tinkering with, I usually win out.

*for others'
sake*

Act happy

*you'll slowly
become
happy*

---

from the writings of DALE CARNEGIE

THE SMALL BOY whistles merrily and loudly when he walks past the cemetery on a dark night in order to bolster up his courage. And generally he overcomes his fear of walking past cemeteries because he has "whistled" up his courage. How many of us, when we're feeling down in the dumps, sing to make other people happy? And in acting happy, we suddenly discover that we're feeling happy. This same principle applies to enthusiasm. If we simulate animation and excitement for our work or the talk we are going to make, we will usually find that we've "simulated" ourselves right into the middle of the kind of emotional drive we're seeking.

GENERAL OMAR BRADLEY

BRAVERY IS THE capacity to perform properly even when scared half to death.

HENRY DAVID THOREAU

IF ONE ADVANCES confidently in the direction of his dreams and endeavors to live the life which he has imagined, he will meet with a success unexpected in common hours. . . . If you have built castles in the air, your work need not be lost; that is where they should be. Now put the foundations under them.

from the writings of DALE CARNEGIE

WE CAN ALL endure disaster and tragedy, and triumph over them—if we have to. We may not think we can, but we have surprisingly strong inner resources that will see us through if we will only make use of them. We are stronger than we think.

◄§WILLIAM JAMES

TO FEEL BRAVE, act as if we were brave, use all of our will to that end, and a courage fit will very likely replace the fit of fear.

◄§RALPH WALDO EMERSON

THEY CAN CONQUER who believe they can. . . . He has not learned the first lesson of life who does not every day surmount a fear.

◄§ELBERT HUBBARD

NO ONE EVER gets very far unless he accomplishes the impossible at least once a day.

◄§ÉMILE COUÉ

IF YOU PERSUADE yourself that you can do a certain thing, provided this thing be possible, you will do it, however difficult it may be. If, on the contrary, you imagine that you cannot do the simplest thing in the world, it is impossible for you to do it, and molehills become for you unscalable mountains.

THOMAS E. WILSON

THIS IS THE foundation of success nine times out of ten—having confidence in yourself and applying yourself with all your might to your work.

RUDYARD KIPLING

If you can dream and not make dreams your master;
If you can think and not make thoughts your aim;
If you can meet with triumph and disaster;
And treat those two impostors just the same,

If you can force your heart, and nerve, and sinew
To serve your turn long after they are gone;
And so hold on when there is nothing in you
Except the will which says to them, "Hold on,"

If you can fill the unforgiving minute
With sixty seconds' worth of distance run,
Yours is the earth and everything that's in it,
And, what is more, you'll be a man, my son.

EDWARD HENRY HARRIMAN

IT IS NEVER safe to look into the future with eyes of fear.

JOHANN WOLFGANG VON GOETHE

What you can do, or dream you can, begin it.
Boldness has genius, power and magic in it.

from the writings of DALE CARNEGIE

IF YOU HAVE FEARS, stop to realize that others have had them too. Probably a fear is haunting you at this moment: the fear of what someone is going to say about you; what the boss is going to do; what the neighbors are going to think. These all have to do with the future. You never fear the past, for you know what has happened and generally it wasn't so bad after all. But the future! Fortunately there is a simple way of fighting fear. Analyze your fear and it will lessen. You will know the worst that can happen and will not be so terrified by it. You will say to yourself, "Why, I can stand that."

ELEANOR ROOSEVELT

I CRAVED ATTENTION all through my childhood, because I was made to feel so conscious of the fact that nothing about me would ever attract attention or bring me admiration. I was told that I would never have the beaux that the rest of the girls in the family had had because I was the ugly duckling . . .

I was ashamed because I had to wear made-over dresses from clothes that my aunts had worn . . . ashamed because I couldn't dance and skate perfectly as others did . . . ashamed because I was different from other girls, ashamed because I was a wallflower. I still remember how thankful I was because a certain boy once asked me for a dance at one of those Christmas parties. His name was Franklin D. Roosevelt.

For over twenty years I was devastated by self-consciousness and fear. My mother and grandmother and my aunts had been famous beauties in New York society, and I was ashamed to be the first girl in our family who was not a belle. My mother would sometimes say to visitors, "Eleanor is such a funny child; so old-fashioned that we call her 'Granny.' "

The big thing that eventually gave me courage was helping people who were worse off than myself. For example, in 1910, my husband was a member of the New York State Senate, and he and eighteen other Assemblymen were waging a war against Tammany Hall. These Assemblymen spent much of their time holding conferences in our home in Albany both day and night. So I visited the wives of these men. I was shocked to find that many of them were spending their days and nights in lonely hotel rooms. They knew no one in Albany except their husbands. . . . I found that by trying to cheer them up and by trying to give them courage, I developed my own courage and self-confidence.

Fear is the most devastating emotion on earth. I fought it and conquered it by helping people who were worse off than I was. I believe that anyone can conquer fear by doing the things he fears to do, provided he keeps doing them until he gets a record of successful experiences behind him.

PUBLILIUS SYRUS

COURAGE COMES BY being brave; fear comes by holding back.

HENRI FAUCONNIER

IN THE LAST resort nothing is ridiculous except the fear of being so.

from the writings of DALE CARNEGIE

THERE IS ONLY one person who can cure someone of self-consciousness, and that is himself. I know of no other handicap the cure for which can be written in so few words—"Forget yourself." When you are feeling shy, timid, self-conscious, put your mind on something else immediately. If you are speaking, forget everything but the subject. Never mind what others are thinking of you or your delivery: Just forget yourself and go ahead.

ANONYMOUS

HE THAT LOSES money loses little, he that loses health loses much, but he that loses courage loses all.

SENECA

OUR FEARS ARE always more numerous than our dangers.

HELEN KELLER

OUR WILL TO act becomes vigorous in proportion to the frequency and definiteness of our actions, and the brain grows to its exercise. Then truly it implements faith. When we let a resolution or a fine emotion dissipate without results, it means more than lost opportunity; it actually retards the fulfillment of future purposes and chills sensibility. There is plenty of courage among us for the abstract but not enough for the concrete, because we allow our daily bits of bravery to evaporate.

⸫DOUGLAS MACARTHUR

THIS GREAT NATION of ours was never more powerful—never more prepared to extend a dynamic and courageous leadership to guide the world through the morass of artificially created timidity, complexity and indecision—it never had less reason for fear. It was never more able to meet the exacting tests of leadership in peace or in war, spiritually, physically or materially. As it is yet unconquered, so it is unconquerable. Its history still lies ahead. Our finest hours are yet to come.

Let us regain some of the courage and faith of the architects who charted the course to our past greatness. Let us look up as befits the most powerful nation on earth, both spiritually and physically.

⸫THEODORE ROOSEVELT

PERHAPS THERE IS no more important component of character than steadfast resolution. The boy who is going to make a great man, or is going to count in any way in after life, must make up his mind not merely to overcome a thousand obstacles, but to win in spite of a thousand repulses and defeats.

---

from the writings of DALE CARNEGIE

YOU CAN CONQUER almost any fear if you will only make up your mind to do so. For remember, fear doesn't exist anywhere except in the mind.

ROBERT W. SERVICE

When you're lost in the wild, and you're scared
    as a child,
And death looks you bang in the eye,
And you're sore as a boil, it's according to Hoyle
To cock your revolver and . . . die.
But the code of a man says: "Fight all you can,"
And self-dissolution is barred.
In hunger and woe, oh, it's easy to blow . . .
It's the hell-served-for-breakfast that's hard.

You're sick of the game! "Well, now, that's a shame."
You're young and you're brave and you're bright.
"You've had a raw deal!" I know—but don't squeal.
Buck up, do your damnedest, and fight.
It's the plugging away that will win you the day,
So don't be a piker, old pard!
Just draw on your grit; it's so easy to quit:
It's the keeping-your-chin-up that's hard.

It's easy to cry that you're beaten—and die.
It's easy to crawfish and crawl;
But to fight and to fight when hope's out of sight,
Why, that's the best game of them all!
And though you come out of each grueling bout
All broken and beaten and scarred,
Just have one more try—it's dead easy to die,
It's the keeping-on-living that's hard.

from the writings of DALE CARNEGIE

WHEN YOU'RE AFRAID, keep your mind on what you have to do. And if you have been thoroughly prepared, you will not be afraid.

THEODORE ROOSEVELT

HAVING BEEN A rather sickly and awkward boy, I was, as a young man, at first both nervous and distrustful of my own prowess. I had to train myself painfully and laboriously not merely as regards my body but as regards my soul and spirit. . . . When a boy, I read a passage in one of Marryat's books which always impressed me. In this passage the captain of some small British man-of-war is explaining to the hero how to acquire the quality of fearlessness. He says that at the outset almost every man is frightened when he goes into action but that the course to follow is for the man to keep such a grip on himself that he can act just as if he were not frightened. After this is kept up long enough, it changes from pretense to reality, and the man does in very fact become fearless by sheer dint of practicing fearlessness when he does not feel it.

This was the theory upon which I went. There were all kinds of things of which I was afraid at first, ranging from grizzly bears to "mean" horses and gun-fighters; but by acting as if I was not afraid I gradually ceased to be afraid. Most men can have the same experience if they choose.

from the writings of DALE CARNEGIE

NATURALNESS IS the easiest thing in the world to acquire, if you will but forget yourself—forget about the impression you are trying to make.

ELBERT HUBBARD

WHENEVER YOU GO out of doors, draw the chin in, carry the crown of the head high, and fill the lungs to the utmost; drink in the sunshine; greet your friends with a smile, and put soul into every handclasp. Do not fear being misunderstood and do not waste a minute thinking about your enemies. Try to fix firmly in your mind what you would like to do; and then, without veering of direction, you will move straight to the goal. Keep your mind on the great and splendid things you would like to do, and then, as the days go gliding by, you will find yourself unconsciously seizing upon the opportunities that are required for the fulfillment of your desire, just as the coral insect takes from the running tide the element it needs. Picture in your mind the able, earnest, useful person you desire to be, and the thought you hold is hourly transforming you into that particular individual. Thought is supreme. Preserve a right mental attitude—the attitude of courage, frankness and good cheer. To think rightly is to create. All things come through desire and every sincere prayer is answered. We become like that on which our hearts are fixed. Carry your chin in and the crown of your head high. We are gods in the chrysalis.

NAPOLEON

IMPOSSIBLE IS A word only to be found in the dictionary of fools.

RALPH WALDO EMERSON

DO THE THING you fear, and the death of fear is certain.

MARTIN LUTHER

EVERYTHING THAT IS done in the world is done by hope. No husbandman would sow one grain of corn if he hoped not it would grow up and become seed; no bachelor would marry a wife if he hoped not to have children; no merchant or tradesman would set himself to work if he did not hope to reap benefit thereby.

MATTHEW 17:20

IF YE HAVE faith as a grain of mustard seed, ye shall say unto this mountain, Remove hence to yonder place; and it shall remove; and nothing shall be impossible unto you.

CONFUCIUS

OUR GREATEST GLORY is not in never falling, but in rising every time we fall.

LORD CHESTERFIELD

FIRMNESS OF PURPOSE is one of the most necessary sinews of character, and one of the best instruments of success. Without it genius wastes its efforts in a maze of inconsistencies.

from the writings of DALE CARNEGIE

TAKE A CHANCE! All life is a chance. The man who goes furthest is generally the one who is willing to do and dare. The "sure thing" boat never gets far from shore.

AUGUST VON SCHLEGEL

IN ACTUAL LIFE every great enterprise begins with and takes its first forward step in faith.

WILLIAM JAMES

IN HUMAN LIFE, although we only see our world, yet encompassing [it] a still wider world may be there; and to believe in that world may be the most essential function that our lives in this world have to perform. The "scientific" life itself has much to do with maybes, and human life at large has everything to do with them. Not a victory is gained, not a deed of faithfulness or courage is done, except upon a maybe; not a service, not a sally of generosity, not a scientific exploration or experiment or textbook, that may not be a mistake. It is only by risking our persons from one hour to another that we live at all. And often enough our faith beforehand in an uncertified result is the only thing that makes the result come true.

SAMUEL BUTLER

FAITH. YOU CAN do very little with it, but you can do nothing without it.

~§SYDNEY SMITH

A GREAT DEAL of talent is lost in the world for want of a little courage. Every day sends to their graves obscure men whom timidity prevented from making a first effort; who, if they could have been induced to begin, would in all probability have gone great lengths in the career of fame. The fact is that to do anything in the world worth doing, we must not stand back shivering and thinking of the cold and danger, but jump in and scramble through as well as we can. It will not do to be perpetually calculating risks and adjusting nice changes; it did very well before the Flood, when a man would consult his friends upon an intended publication for a hundred and fifty years, and live to see his success afterward; but at present, a man waits, and doubts, and consults his brother, and his particular friends, till one day he finds he is sixty years old and that he has lost so much time in consulting cousins and friends that he has no more time to follow their advice.

~§WINSTON CHURCHILL

COURAGE IS RIGHTLY esteemed the first of human qualities because it is the quality which guarantees all others.

~§RALPH WALDO EMERSON

WHEN A RESOLUTE young fellow steps up to the great bully, the world, and takes him boldly by the beard, he is often surprised to find it comes off in his hand, and that it was only tied on to scare away timid adventurers.

◆(◇(◇(◌)◇)◇)◆

from the writings of DALE CARNEGIE

I F YOU WANT to develop courage, do the thing you fear to do and keep on doing it until you get a record of successful experiences behind you. That is the quickest and surest way ever yet discovered to conquer fear.

⇜§WILLIAM FEATHER

HERE IS THE secret of inspiration. Tell yourself that thousands and tens of people, not very intelligent and certainly no more intelligent than the rest of us, have mastered problems as difficult as those that now baffle you.

⇜§WINSTON CHURCHILL

WE SHALL NOT flag or fail. We shall go on to the end. We shall fight in France, we shall fight on the seas and oceans, we shall fight with growing confidence and growing strength in the air. We shall defend our island, whatever the cost may be. We shall fight on the beaches, we shall fight on the landing-grounds, we shall fight in the fields and in the streets, we shall fight in the hills. We shall never surrender; and even if, which I do not for a moment believe, this island or a large part of it were subjugated and starving, then our Empire beyond the seas, armed and guarded by the British Fleet, would carry on the struggle, until, in God's good time, the New World, with all its power and might, steps forth to rescue and liberation of the old.

from the writings of DALE CARNEGIE

THE NEXT TIME you are appalled by some task, sail into it, accomplish the impossible. It can be done; if you will have the utmost confidence in yourself, you can do it.

SAMUEL JOHNSON

SELF-CONFIDENCE IS the first requisite to great undertakings.

THEODORE ROOSEVELT

NO MAN IS worth his salt who is not ready at all times to risk his body, to risk his well-being, to risk his life, in a great cause.

THOMAS CARLYLE

THE COURAGE WE desire and prize is not the courage to die decently, but to live manfully.

MICHEL EYQUEM DE MONTAIGNE

HE WHO FEARS he will suffer, already suffers because of his fear.

BENJAMIN DISRAELI

ACTION MAY NOT always bring happiness; but there is no happiness without action.

✑ EDDIE RICKENBACKER

NO ONE SHOULD fear death. I know, because I have come face to face with death several times. It is really a pleasant experience. You seem to hear beautiful music and everything is mellow and sweet and serene—no struggle, no terror, just calmness and beauty. When death comes, you will find it to be one of the easiest and most blissful experiences you have ever had.

✑ MARTIN LUTHER

AS WISDOM WITHOUT courage is futile, even so faith without hope is nothing worth; for hope endures and overcomes misfortune and evil.

✑ WINSTON CHURCHILL

IT IS VERY much better sometimes to have a panic feeling beforehand, and then be quite calm when things happen, than to be extremely calm beforehand and to get into a panic when things happen.

from the writings of DALE CARNEGIE

THE WAY TO defeat fear: decide on a course of conduct and follow it. Keep so busy and work so hard that you forget about being afraid.

from the writings of DALE CARNEGIE

M<small>OST OF US</small> have far more courage than we ever dreamed we possessed.

FRANÇOIS DE LA ROCHEFOUCAULD

<small>PERFECT COURAGE IS</small> to do unwitnessed what we should be capable of doing before all the world.

MARK TWAIN

<small>COURAGE IS RESISTANCE</small> to fear, mastery of fear—not absence of fear. Except a creature be part coward it is not a compliment to say it is brave; it is merely a loose misapplication of the word. Consider the flea!—incomparably the bravest of all the creatures of God, if ignorance of fear were courage. Whether you are asleep or awake he will attack you, caring nothing for the fact that in bulk and strength you are to him as are the massed armies of the earth to a sucking child; he lives both day and night and all days and nights in the very lap of peril and the immediate presence of death, and yet is no more afraid than is the man who walks the streets of a city that was threatened by an earthquake ten centuries before. When we speak of Clive, Nelson and Putnam as men who "didn't know what fear was," we ought always to add the flea—and put him at the head of the procession.

~§ROBERT HILLYER

> If the Sun and Moon should doubt,
> They'd immediately go out.

A s a poet, I have often wished I could have written these lines of William Blake's. As a teacher, I have often called them to my aid for the encouragement of someone who could not get started on a project. Faith in oneself is an important part of all other faiths. The lack of it can paralyze a life.

Of course it is natural to have nervous moments. Everyone who has spoken in public is acquainted with the panic that seizes one just before the occasion, and we are told that the best actors are those who are most nervous just before the curtain goes up. There is always the fear that lines will be forgotten, that something will go wrong, and yet the play goes on, usually without a hitch.

The same preliminary lack of confidence attends every accomplishment known to man, the launching of a military campaign, the composition of a poem, the salesman's first trip, the bride's cookery. But if we all succumbed to such misgivings, nothing would ever be done.

Self-doubt is caused by the fact that every human activity involves some other person whose praise or blame seems unduly important. We set a goal of perfection before ourselves and groaningly conclude that it cannot be achieved.

But perfectionism is a dangerous state of mind in an imperfect world. The best way is to forget doubts and set about the task in hand. While the battle is being fought or the cake is baking in the oven, leave the outcome to the future where it belongs. If you are doing your best, you will not have time to worry about failure.

---

from the writings of DALE CARNEGIE

FACE THE THING that seems overwhelming and you will be surprised how your fear will melt away.

HARRIET BEECHER STOWE

WHEN YOU GET into a tight place and everything goes against you, till it seems as though you could not hold on a minute longer, never give up then, for that is just the place and time that the tide will turn.

WINSTON CHURCHILL

HOWEVER TEMPTING IT might be to some when much trouble lies ahead to step aside adroitly and put someone else up to take the blows, I do not intend to take that cowardly course, but, on the contrary, to stand to my post and persevere in accordance with my duty as I see it.

HENRY WADSWORTH LONGFELLOW

Be still, sad heart, and cease repining,
Behind the clouds the sun is shining;
Thy fate is the common fate of all;
Into each life some rain must fall,—
Some days must be dark and dreary.

———————◆(◆(◆(◆(◇)◆)◆)◆————————

from the writings of D A L E   C A R N E G I E

To conquer fear and worry, keep busy!

—————————————————————————————

⌁LLOYD JONES

THE MEN WHO try to do something and fail are infinitely better than those who try to do nothing and succeed.

⌁WINSTON CHURCHILL

THE TIME TO be frightened is when evils can be remedied; when they cannot be fully remedied they must be faced with courage.

⌁ANONYMOUS

LUCK IS A very good word if you put a *P* before it.

⌁WILLIAM GLADSTONE

NO MAN EVER became great or good except through many and great mistakes.

⌁FREDERICK ROBERTSON

TO BELIEVE IS to be strong. Doubt cramps energy. Belief is power.

RALPH WALDO EMERSON

EVERY GREAT AND commanding moment in the annals of the world is the triumph of some enthusiasm.

WINSTON CHURCHILL

I WOULD SAY to the House, as I said to those who have joined this Government: "I have nothing to offer but blood, toil, tears and sweat." We have before us an ordeal of the most grievous kind. We have before us many, many long months of struggle and suffering.

You ask: "What is our policy?" I will say: "It is to wage war by sea, land, and air with all the strength that God can give us: to wage war against a monstrous tyranny, never surpassed in the dark lamentable catalogue of human crime." That is our policy.

You ask: "What is our aim?" I can answer in one word: "Victory!" Victory at all costs, victory in spite of all terror, victory however long and hard the road may be; for without victory there is no survival.

from the writings of DALE CARNEGIE

FEAR IS A BULLY and a coward and all we have to do to conquer fear is to forget that it is there. You can do it.

⋐FREDERICK WILLIAMSON

THE LONGER I live the more certain I am that enthusiasm is the most important of all traits or qualifications. The difference in actual skill and ability and intelligence between the man who succeeds and the man who fails usually is not very great. But if there are two men starting out with equal ability and intelligence, physical strength and the other important qualifications, the man who is enthusiastic is the one who is going to come in first. And often a man with second-rate ability will outstrip a very capable man if he has enthusiasm and the first-rater hasn't.

⋐WILLIAM MAKEPEACE THACKERAY

TO LOVE AND win is the best thing; to love and lose the next best.

---

from the writings of DALE CARNEGIE

YOU ARE NEVER defeated as long as you don't think the job is impossible.

⋐JAMES GARFIELD

IF WRINKLES MUST be written upon our brows, let them not be written upon the heart. The spirit should not grow old.

⋐JOHANN WOLFGANG VON GOETHE

THE IMPORTANT THING in life is to have a great aim and to possess the aptitude and the perseverance to attain it.

from the writings of DALE CARNEGIE

THE VERY BEST way in all the world to overcome self-consciousness and shyness is to get interested in other people and to think of them and, almost miraculously, your timidity will pass. Do something for other people. Practice deeds of kindness, acts of friendliness, and you'll be surprised to see what happens.

WOODROW WILSON

WITHOUT ENTHUSIASM THERE is no progress in the world.

SIR WILLIAM OSLER

THE VERY FIRST step toward success in any occupation is to become interested in it.

WALTER BAGEHOT

STRONG BELIEFS WIN strong men, and then make them stronger.

CHARLES SCHWAB

A MAN CAN succeed at almost anything for which he has unlimited enthusiasm.

THOMAS A. EDISON

WHEN A MAN dies, if he can pass enthusiasm along to his children, he has left them an estate of incalculable value.

⋙SIR WILLIAM OSLER

NO MAN IS really happy or safe without a hobby and it makes precious little difference what the outside interest may be—botany, beetles or butterflies; roses, tulips or irises; fishing, mountaineering or antiquities—anything will do so long as he straddles a hobby and rides it hard.

⋙LOUISA MAY ALCOTT

FAR AWAY THERE in the sunshine are my highest aspirations. I may not reach them, but I can look up and see their beauty, believe in them, and try to follow where they lead.

⋙ELBERT HUBBARD

ENTHUSIASM IS LIKE having two right hands.

⋙EDWARD BULWER-LYTTON

NOTHING IS SO contagious as enthusiasm. It is the real allegory of the tale of Orpheus; it moves stones and charms brutes. It is the genius of sincerity and truth accomplishes no victories without it.

---

from the writings of DALE CARNEGIE

INACTION BREEDS DOUBT and fear. Action breeds confidence and courage. If you want to conquer fear, don't sit at home and think about it. Go out and get busy.

from the writings of DALE CARNEGIE

TAKE STOCK of your fears now and see how many of them are senseless. If you are honest with yourself you will probably find that most of them are groundless.

CHARLES KINGSLEY

WE ACT AS though comfort and luxury were the chief requirements of life, when all that we need to make us really happy is something to be enthusiastic about.

JONATHAN OGDEN ARMOUR

IF YOU WOULD like to be a power among men, cultivate enthusiasm. People will like you better for it; you will escape the dull routine of a mechanical existence and you will make headway wherever you are. It cannot be otherwise, for this is the human life. Put your soul into your work and not only will you find it pleasanter every hour of the day, but people will believe in you just as they believe in electricity when they get into touch with a dynamo.

MATTHEW ARNOLD

NO ONE CAN give faith, unless he has faith; the persuaded persuade.

THEODORE ROOSEVELT

IN LIFE, AS in a football game, the principle to follow is: Hit the line hard; don't foul and don't shirk, but hit the line hard.

from the writings of DALE CARNEGIE

DEVELOP SUCCESS from failures. Discouragement and failure are two of the surest steppingstones to success. No other element can do so much for a man if he is willing to study them and make capital out of them. Look backward. Can't you see where your failures have helped you?

W. C. HOLMAN

GENIUS IS INTENSITY. The man who gets anything worth having is the man who goes after his object as a bulldog goes after a cat— with every fiber in him tense with eagerness and determination.

H. ADDINGTON BRUCE

THE MAN OR woman of enthusiastic trend always exercises a magnetic influence over those with whom he or she comes in contact.

RUSSELL H. CONWELL

BE INTENSELY IN earnest. Enthusiasm invites enthusiasm.

JOHN G. SHEDD

I LIKE THE man who bubbles over with enthusiasm. Better be a geyser than a mud puddle.

MARTIN LUTHER

IF I WISH to compose or write or pray or preach well, I must be angry. Then all the blood in my veins is stirred, and my understanding is sharpened.

SECOND CHRONICLES

HE DID IT with all his heart and prospered.

WALTER H. COTTINGHAM

MERIT BEGETS CONFIDENCE, confidence begets enthusiasm, enthusiasm conquers the world.

WILLIAM HAZLITT

HONESTY IS ONE part of eloquence; we persuade others by being in earnest ourselves.

from the writings of DALE CARNEGIE

DO THINGS for others and you'll find your self-consciousness evaporating like morning dew on a Missouri cornfield in July.

from the writings of DALE CARNEGIE

EVERYONE should have a deep-seated interest, or hobby, to enrich his mind, add zest to living, and perhaps, depending upon what it is, result in a service to his country.

FREDERICK B. ROBINSON

I BELIEVE that the intense purpose, the moral integrity, the self-loyalty that makes a man carry through whatever he undertakes, is the biggest single factor in fitting his mind for great accomplishments.

ABRAHAM LINCOLN

IF YOU ARE resolutely determined to make a lawyer of yourself, the thing is more than half done already. . . . Always bear in mind that your own resolution to succeed is more important than any other one thing.

EUGENE GRACE

DO ONE THING at a time, and do that one thing as if your life depended upon it.

RALPH WALDO EMERSON

KNOW THE FACT—hug the fact. For the essential thing is heat, and heat comes from sincerity.

⋐§IRVING BERLIN

YOU CAN'T WRITE a song out of thin air. You have to know and feel what you are writing about.

⋐§ELBERT HUBBARD

THE WORLD BESTOWS its big prizes both in money and honors for but one thing. And that is initiative. And what is initiative? I'll tell you: it is doing the right thing without being told.

⋐§VISCOUNT JOHN MORLEY

TO KNOW WHEN one's self is interested, is the first condition of interesting other people.

⋐§JOSEPH TUCKERMAN

LET US RECOGNIZE the beauty and power of true enthusiasm; and whatever we may do to enlighten ourselves or others, guard against checking or chilling a single earnest sentiment.

---

from the writings of DALE CARNEGIE

IF YOU WANT to conquer fear, don't think about yourself. Try to help others, and your fears will vanish.

from the writings of DALE CARNEGIE

ENTHUSIASM IS THE dynamics of your personality. Without it, whatever abilities you may possess lie dormant; and it is safe to say that nearly every man has more latent power than he ever learns to use. You may have knowledge, sound judgment, good reasoning faculties; but no one—not even yourself—will know it until you discover how to put your heart into thought and action.

BENJAMIN DISRAELI

EVERY PRODUCTION OF genius must be the production of enthusiasm.

HORACE

IF YOU WISH to draw tears from me, you must first feel pain yourself.

BERNARD BARUCH

I WAS THE son of an immigrant. I experienced bigotry, intolerance and prejudice, even as so many of you have. Instead of allowing these things to embitter me, I took them as spurs to more strenuous effort.

~§JOHN DEWEY

FAILURE IS INSTRUCTIVE. The person who really thinks learns quite as much from his failures as from his successes.

~§JOHN D. ROCKEFELLER

I ALWAYS TRIED to turn every disaster into an opportunity.

~§HARRY EMERSON FOSDICK

THERE IS A Scandinavian saying which some of us might well take as a rallying cry for our lives: "The north wind made the Vikings." Wherever did we get the idea that secure and pleasant living, the absence of difficulty, and the comfort of ease, ever of themselves made people either good or happy? Upon the contrary, people who pity themselves go on pitying themselves even when they are laid softly on a cushion, but always in history character and happiness have come to people in all sorts of circumstances, good, bad and indifferent, when they shouldered their personal responsibility. So, repeatedly the north wind had made the Vikings.

———————⊰⟨⊰⟨⊰⟨⟨⟪⊂⟩⊳⟩⊳⟩⊳⟩⊱———————

from the writings of DALE CARNEGIE

THIS IS THE day of dramatization. Merely stating a truth isn't enough. The truth has to be made vivid, interesting, dramatic. You have to use showmanship. The movies do it. Radio does it. And you will have to do it if you want attention.

⋅§HELEN KELLER

GRIEF AND PAIN are but the soil from which springs the lovely plant—unselfishness. Be gentle and learn how to suffer. . . . Whatever you can do to live bravely—without impatience or repining—will help you to live some day in joyful contentment.

⋅§LORD BYRON

ADVERSITY IS THE first path to truth. He who hath proved war, storm, or woman's rage, whether his winters be eighteen or eighty, hath won the experience which is deemed so weighty.

⋅§WILLIAM SHAKESPEARE

Sweet are the uses of adversity,
Which, like the toad, ugly and venomous,
Wears yet a precious jewel in his head.

---

from the writings of DALE CARNEGIE

FLAMING ENTHUSIASM, backed up by horse sense and persistence, is the quality that most frequently makes for success.

---

from the writings of DALE CARNEGIE

How CAN YOU make yourself become enthusiastic? By telling yourself what you like about what you are doing and pass on quickly from the part you don't like to the part you do like. Then act enthusiastic; tell someone about it; let them know why it interests you.

AMOS BRONSON ALCOTT

WE MOUNT TO heaven mostly on the ruins of our cherished schemes, finding our failures were successes.

GERMAN PROVERB

WHO HAS NEVER tasted what is bitter does not know what is sweet.

HENRY J. KAISER

PROBLEMS ARE ONLY opportunities in work clothes.

WILLIAM CULLEN BRYANT

DIFFICULTY, MY BRETHREN, is the nurse of greatness—a harsh nurse, who roughly rocks her foster-children into strength and athletic proportion.

─────────────◦⟨◦⟨◦⟨◦⟨◦⟩◦⟩◦⟩◦⟩◦────────────

from the writings of DALE CARNEGIE

ENTHUSIASM IS NOT merely an outward expression. It works from within. Enthusiasm is born of a genuine liking for some phase of what you are doing.

───────────────────────────────────────

WILLIAM WHEWELL

EVERY FAILURE IS a step to success; every detection of what is false directs us toward what is true; every trial exhausts some tempting form of error. Not only so, but scarcely any attempt is entirely a failure; scarcely any theory, the result of steady thought, is altogether false; no tempting form of error is without some latent charm derived from truth.

JOHN KEATS

FAILURE IS, IN a sense, the highway to success, inasmuch as every discovery of what is false leads us to seek earnestly after what is true, and every fresh experience points out some form of error which we shall afterward carefully avoid.

BENJAMIN DISRAELI

THERE IS NO education like adversity.

PROVERBS: OLD TESTAMENT

IF THOU FAINT in the day of adversity, thy strength is small.

WILLIAM BOLITHO

THE MOST IMPORTANT thing in life is not to capitalize on your gains. Any fool can do that. The really important thing is to profit from your losses. That requires intelligence; and it makes the difference between a man of sense and a fool.

WASHINGTON IRVING

GREAT MINDS HAVE purposes, others have wishes. Little minds are tamed and subdued by misfortune; but great minds rise above them.

PLUTARCH

THE MEASURE OF a man is the way he bears up under misfortune.

---

from the writings of DALE CARNEGIE

THE WAY TO acquire enthusiasm is to believe in what you are doing and in yourself and to want to get something definite accomplished. Enthusiasm will follow as night the day.

——————————◄(◄(◄(◄(◌)◄)◄)◄)◄——————————

from the writings of DALE CARNEGIE

YOU CAN'T GET anywhere in this world without *wanting* to do something.

►HARRY EMERSON FOSDICK

THAT IS LIFE, to have your A-string snap and finish on three strings.

►FRANÇOIS DE LA ROCHEFOUCAULD

THERE ARE NO accidents so unfortunate from which skillful men will not draw some advantage, nor so fortunate that foolish men will not turn them to their hurt.

►WILLIAM HAZLITT

PROSPERITY IS A GREAT teacher; adversity is a greater. Possession pampers the mind; privation trains and strengthens it.

►HENRY WARD BEECHER

IT IS DEFEAT that turns bones to flint; it is defeat that turns gristle to muscle; it is defeat that makes men invincible.

►WENDELL PHILLIPS

WHAT IS DEFEAT? Nothing but education, nothing but the first step to something better.

◄§SIR THOMAS BROWNE

LIGHT THAT MAKES some things seen, makes some things invisible. Were it not for darkness and the shadow of the earth, the noblest part of the Creation would remain unseen, and the stars in heaven invisible.

2

Dale Carnegie wrote his book *How to Stop Worrying and Start Living* in order to show that life is very much what we make it. Since life is a day-to-day affair, we shouldn't underestimate the importance of each day, or let the worries of one day ruin the next. Faith—faith in God, in the future, in our neighbors and in ourselves—will sustain us under stress. ❧

---

from the writings of DALE CARNEGIE

I F YOU HAVE a worry problem, do these three things:

([1. Ask yourself, "What is the worst that can possibly happen?"

([2. Prepare to accept it if you have to.

([3. Then calmly proceed to improve on the worst.

⊷§ JAMES GORDON GILKEY

W HAT IS THE true picture of your life? Imagine that there is an hourglass on your desk. Connecting the bowl at the top with the bowl at the bottom is a tube so thin that only one grain of sand can pass through it at a time.

That is the true picture of your life, even on a super-busy day. The crowded hours come to you always one moment at a time. That is the only way they can come. The day may bring many tasks, many problems, strains, but invariably they come in single file.

49

from the writings of DALE CARNEGIE

WHY DOES SUCH a simple thing as keeping busy help to drive out anxiety? Because of a law—one of the most fundamental laws ever revealed by psychology. And that law is: that it is utterly impossible for any human mind, no matter how brilliant, to think of more than one thing at any given time.

JACK DEMPSEY

BY FORGETTING THE past and by throwing myself into other interests, I forget to worry.

GENERAL GEORGE C. MARSHALL

WHEN A THING is done, it's done. Don't look back. Look forward to your next objective.

REINHOLD NIEBUHR

God grant me the serenity
To accept the things I cannot change,
The courage to change the things I can;
And the wisdom to know the difference.

HERBERT HOOVER

NEVER WORRY ABOUT anything that is past. Charge it up to experience and forget the trouble. There are always plenty of troubles ahead, so don't turn and look back on any behind you.

from the writings of DALE CARNEGIE

IF YOU AND I don't keep busy—if we sit around and brood—we will hatch out a whole flock of what Charles Darwin used to call the "wibber gibbers." And the "wibber gibbers" are nothing but old-fashioned gremlins that will run us hollow and destroy our power of action and our power of will.

⋖ BLAISE PASCAL

TIME CURES SORROWS and squabbles because we all change, and are no longer the same persons. Neither the offender nor the offended is the same.

⋖ HENRY WADSWORTH LONGFELLOW

The night shall be filled with music
And the cares that infest the day
Shall fold their tents like the Arabs,
And silently steal away.

⋖ NAPOLEON

WHEN I WANT to consider a particular problem, I open a certain drawer. When I have settled the matter in my mind, I close that drawer and open another. When I desire to sleep, I close all the drawers.

⋖ SAMUEL JOHNSON

HOW INSIGNIFICANT THIS will appear a twelve-month hence.

from the writings of DALE CARNEGIE

ABOUT NINETY per cent of the things in our lives are right and about ten per cent are wrong. If we want to be happy, all we have to do is to concentrate on the ninety per cent that are right and ignore the ten per cent that are wrong. If we want to be worried and bitter and have stomach ulcers, all we have to do is to concentrate on the ten per cent that are wrong and ignore the ninety per cent that are glorious.

OVID

HAPPY IS THE man who has broken the chains which hurt the mind, and has given up worrying once and for all.

SIR WILLIAM OSLER

SHUT OUT ALL of your past except that which will help you weather your tomorrows.

ELBERT HUBBARD

WORRY KILLS MORE people than work—because more people tackle it.

FRANCIS BACON

THAT WHICH IS past is gone and irrevocable, and wise men have enough to do with things present and to come; therefore they do but trifle with themselves that labor in past matters.

SIR WILLIAM OSLER

"UNDRESS," AS GEORGE HERBERT says, "your soul at night," not by self-examination, but by shedding, as you do your garments, the daily sins whether of omission or commission, and you will wake a free man, with a new life.

WILLIAM SHAKESPEARE

PRESENT FEARS ARE less than horrible imaginings.

JAMES RUSSELL LOWELL

LET US BE of good cheer, remembering that the misfortunes hardest to bear are those which never happen.

MARSHAL FERDINAND FOCH

I KNOW THAT I am considered an inveterate optimist and properly so. Why? Because I always turn my eyes toward success, not failure. I involuntarily turn my back on disaster and eliminate the hypothesis of failure. This is my philosophy in action. Every time you have a task before you, examine it carefully, take exact measure of what is expected of you. Then make your plan and, in order to execute it properly, create for yourself a method, never improvise.

---

from the writings of DALE CARNEGIE

OUR FATIGUE IS often caused not by work, but by worry, frustration and resentment.

from the writings of DALE CARNEGIE

ALL THE KING'S horses and all the king's men can't put the past together again. So let's remember: Don't try to saw sawdust.

✑JULIUS ROSENWALD

EARLY IN MY business career I learned the folly of worrying about anything. I have always worked as hard as I could, but when a thing went wrong and could not be righted, I dismissed it from my mind.

✑HENRY WARD BEECHER

WHEN I HAVE something that causes me concern, I just dismiss everything connected with it from my mind and let my work absorb me. It's surprising how it clears up.

✑WINSTON CHURCHILL

LET OUR ADVANCE worrying become advance thinking and planning.

✑VICTOR HUGO

HAVE COURAGE FOR the great sorrows of life and patience for the small ones; and when you have laboriously accomplished your daily task, go to sleep in peace. God is awake.

❧JOSH BILLINGS

IT IS THE little bits of things that fret and worry us; we can dodge an elephant, but we can't a fly.

❧HENRY WARD BEECHER

IT IS NOT work that kills men; it is worry. Work is healthy; you can hardly put more upon a man than he can bear. Worry is rust upon the blade. It is not the revolution that destroys the machinery but the friction.

❧CHARLES F. KETTERING

A PROBLEM WELL stated is a problem half solved.

❧EDWARD EVERETT HALE

WE SHOULD NEVER attempt to bear more than one kind of trouble at once. Some people bear three kinds—all they have had, all they have now, and all they expect to have.

---

from the writings of DALE CARNEGIE

WHEN WE HATE our enemies, we are giving them power over us: power over our sleep, our appetites, our blood pressure, our health, and our happiness. Our enemies would dance with joy if only they knew how they were worrying us, lacerating us, and getting even with us! Our hate is not hurting them at all, but our hate is turning our own days and nights into a hellish turmoil.

from the writings of DALE CARNEGIE

PUT A BIG, broad, honest-to-God smile on your face; throw back your shoulders; take a good, deep breath; and sing a snatch of song. If you can't sing, whistle. If you can't whistle, hum. You will quickly discover that it is physically impossible to remain blue or depressed while you are acting out the symptoms of being radiantly happy!

ROGER W. BABSON

WHEN I FIND myself depressed over present conditions, I can, within one hour, banish worry and turn myself into a shouting optimist.

Here is how I do it. I enter my library, close my eyes, and walk to certain shelves containing only books on history. With my eyes still shut, I reach for a book, not knowing whether I am picking up Prescott's *Conquest of Mexico* or Suetonius' *Lives of the Twelve Caesars*. With my eyes still closed, I open the book at random. I then open my eyes and read for an hour; and the more I read, the more sharply I realize that the world has always been in the throes of agony, that civilization has always been tottering on the brink. The pages of history fairly shriek with tragic tales of war, famine, poverty, pestilence, and man's inhumanity to man. After reading history for an hour, I realize that bad as conditions are now, they are infinitely better than they used to be. This enables me to see and face my present troubles in their proper perspective as well as to realize that the world as a whole is constantly growing better.

FRANKLIN PIERCE ADAMS

INSOMNIACS DON'T SLEEP because they worry about it, and they worry about it because they don't sleep.

PLAUTUS

PATIENCE IS THE best remedy for every trouble.

DOROTHY DIX

I HAVE BEEN through the depths of poverty and sickness. When people ask me what has kept me going through the troubles that come to all of us, I always reply: "I stood yesterday. I can stand today. And I will not permit myself to think about what might happen tomorrow."

COLONEL EDDIE EAGAN

WHEN I FIND MYSELF worrying and mentally going around in endless circles like a camel turning a water wheel in Egypt, a good physical workout helps me to chase those "blues" away.

I find the best antidote for worry is exercise. Use your muscles more and your brain less when you are worried, and you will be surprised at the result. It works that way with me—worry goes when exercise begins.

SOLON

IF ALL OUR misfortunes were laid in one common heap, whence every one must take an equal portion, most people would be contented to take their own and depart.

from the writings of DALE CARNEGIE

PUT A "STOP-LOSS" order on your worries. Decide just how much anxiety a thing may be worth—and refuse to give it any more.

EPICTETUS

THERE IS ONLY one way to happiness and that is to cease worrying about things which are beyond the power of our will.

JOSEPH R. SIZOO

YEARS AGO, IN a day of uncertainty and disillusionment, when my whole life seemed to be overwhelmed by forces beyond my control, one morning quite casually I opened my New Testament and my eyes fell upon this sentence, "He that sent me is with me—the Father hath not left me alone." My life has never been the same since that hour. Everything for me has been forever different after that. I suppose that not a day has passed that I have not repeated it to myself. Many have come to me for counseling during these years, and I have always sent them away with this sustaining sentence. Ever since that hour when my eyes fell upon it, I have lived by this sentence. I have walked with it and I have found in it my peace and strength. To me it is the very essence of religion. It lies at the rock bottom of everything that makes life worth living. It is the Golden Text of my life.

⚞HARRY EMERSON FOSDICK

ON THE SLOPE of Long's Peak in Colorado lies the ruin of a gigantic tree. Naturalists tell us that it stood for some four hundred years. It was a seedling when Columbus landed at San Salvador, and half grown when the Pilgrims settled at Plymouth. During the course of its long life it was struck by lightning fourteen times, and the innumerable avalanches and storms of four centuries thundered past it. It survived them all. In the end, however, an army of beetles attacked the tree and leveled it to the ground. The insects ate their way through the bark and gradually destroyed the inner strength of the tree by their tiny but incessant attacks. A forest giant which age had not withered, nor lightning blasted, nor storms subdued, fell at last before beetles so small that a man could crush them between his forefinger and his thumb.

---

from the writings of **DALE CARNEGIE**

DON'T FUSS ABOUT trifles. Don't permit little things— the mere termites of life—to ruin your happiness.

⚞THOMAS CARLYLE

OUR MAIN BUSINESS is not to see what lies dimly at a distance, but to do what lies clearly at hand.

⚞HENRY FORD

WHEN I CAN'T handle events, I let them handle themselves.

—◇《◇《◇《○》◇》◇》◇—

from the writings of DALE CARNEGIE

USE THE LAW of averages to outlaw your worries. Ask yourself: "What are the odds against this thing's happening at all?"

⛬WILLIAM JAMES

WHEN ONCE A decision is reached and execution is the order of the day, dismiss absolutely all responsibility and care about the outcome.

⛬BENJAMIN FRANKLIN

LET ALL YOUR things have their places; let each part of your business have its time.

⛬MARCUS AURELIUS

TROUBLE NOT THYSELF by pondering life in its entirety. Strive not to comprehend in one view the nature and number of burdens that, belike, will fall to thy share. Rather, as each occasion arises in the present put this question to thyself: "Where lies the unbearable, unendurable part of this task?" Confession will put thee to the blush! Next recall to mind that neither past nor future can weigh thee down, only the present. And the present will shrink to littleness if thou but set it apart, assign it its boundaries, and then ask thy mind if it avail not to bear even this!

K. T. KELLER

WHEN I AM up against a tough situation, if I can do anything about it, I do it. If I can't, I just forget it. I never worry about the future, because I know no man living can possibly figure out what is going to happen in the future. There are so many forces that will affect that future. Nobody can tell what prompts those forces—or understand them. So why worry about them?

HARRY EMERSON FOSDICK

HATING PEOPLE IS like burning down your own home to get rid of a rat.

J. C. PENNEY

I WOULDN'T WORRY if I lost every dollar I have because I don't see what is to be gained by worrying. I do the best job I possibly can, and leave the results in the laps of the gods.

GEORGE BERNARD SHAW

THE SECRET OF being miserable is to have the leisure to bother about whether you are happy or not.

MOTHER GOOSE RHYME

> For every ailment under the sun,
> There is a remedy, or there is none;
> If there be one, try to find it;
> If there be none, never mind it.

❧ FRANÇOIS DE LA ROCHEFOUCAULD

IT IS BETTER to try to bear the ills we have than to anticipate those which may never come.

❧ GEORGE MACDONALD

IT HAS BEEN well said that no man ever sank under the burden of the day. It is when tomorrow's burden is added to the burden of today that the weight is more than a man can bear.

———————————————————

from the writings of DALE CARNEGIE

A WELL-KNOWN legal maxim says: *De minimis non curat lex*—"The law does not concern itself with trifles." And neither should the worrier—if he wants peace of mind.

❧ BENJAMIN FRANKLIN

DO NOT ANTICIPATE trouble, or worry about what may never happen. Keep in the sunlight.

❧ HENRY WARD BEECHER

WHEN WE BORROW trouble, and look forward into the future and see what storms are coming, and distress ourselves before they come as to how we shall avert them if they ever do come, we lose our proper trustfulness in God. When we torment ourselves with imaginary dangers or trials or reverses, we have already parted with that perfect love which casteth out fear.

from the writings of DALE CARNEGIE

GET THE FACTS. Let's not even attempt to solve our problems without first collecting all the facts in an impartial manner.

THOMAS JEFFERSON

HOW MUCH HAVE cost us the evils that never happened!

WILLIAM COWPER

THE CARES OF today are seldom those of tomorrow; and when we lie down at night we may safely say to most of our troubles, "Ye have done your worst, and we shall see you no more."

ALBERT EINSTEIN

I NEVER THINK of the future. It comes soon enough.

ANDRÉ GIDE

HE WHO WAITS for God fails to understand that he possesses Him. Believe that God and happiness are one, and put all your happiness in the present moment.

HORACE MANN

LOST, YESTERDAY, SOMEWHERE between sunrise and sunset, two golden hours, each set with sixty diamond minutes. No reward is offered for they are gone forever.

64

≈ HONORÉ DE BALZAC

AFTER ALL, OUR worst misfortunes never happen, and most miseries lie in anticipation.

≈ DWIGHT D. EISENHOWER

UNLESS EACH DAY can be looked back upon by an individual as one in which he has had some fun, some joy, some real satisfaction, that day is a loss. It is un-Christian and wicked, in my opinion, to allow such a thing to occur.

---

from the writings of DALE CARNEGIE

WHEN WE HAVE accepted the worst, we have nothing more to lose. And that automatically means—we have everything to gain!

≈ HORACE

Happy the man, and happy he alone,
He, who can call today his own;
He who, secure within, can say:
"Tomorrow, do thy worst, for I have liv'd today."

≈ BENJAMIN FRANKLIN

DO NOT SQUANDER time, for that is the stuff life is made of.

from the writings of DALE CARNEGIE

D<small>O YOU REMEMBER</small> the things you were worrying about a year ago? How did they work out? Didn't you waste a lot of fruitless energy on account of most of them? Didn't most of them turn out all right after all?

GEOFFREY CHAUCER

T<small>HE GOODNESS THAT</small> thou mayest do this day, do it; and . . . delay it not till tomorrow.

RALPH WALDO EMERSON

O<small>F ALL THE</small> ages, the present hour and circumstance is the cumulative result; this is the best throw of the dice of nature that has yet been or that is yet possible.

HENRY DAVID THOREAU

A<small>BOVE ALL, WE</small> cannot afford not to live in the present. He is blessed over all mortals who loses no moment of the passing life in remembering the past.

SAMUEL BUTLER

O<small>UR LATEST MOMENT</small> is always our supreme moment. Five minutes' delay in dinner now is more important than a great sorrow ten years gone.

─────────────────◆〈◆〈◆〈C〉◆〉◆〉◆───────────────────

from the writings of DALE CARNEGIE

L OOK FACTS IN the face, bitter though they may be: make a decision, and after you have once made the decision, devote all your time to carrying it out. Don't spend any time worrying about whether or not it is right. Make it right!

──

✒ALFRED, LORD TENNYSON

THE TENDER GRACE of a day that is dead will never come back to me.

✒HENRY L. MENCKEN

WE ARE HERE and it is now; further than that all human knowledge is moonshine.

✒JOHANN WOLFGANG VON GOETHE

ALWAYS HOLD FAST to the present hour. Every state of duration, every second, is of infinite value. . . . I have staked on the present as one stakes a large sum on one card, and I have sought without exaggerating to make it as high as possible.

✒DAVID GRAYSON

I THINK IT truth that a life uncommanded now is uncommanded; a life unenjoyed now is unenjoyed; a life not lived wisely now is not lived wisely; for the past is gone and no one knows the future.

from the writings of DALE CARNEGIE

IF YOU WERE to read everything that has ever been written about worry by the great philosophers of the universe, you would never read anything more profound than "Don't cross your bridges until you come to them" and "Don't cry over spilt milk."

JONATHAN SWIFT

VERY FEW MEN, properly speaking, live at present, but are providing to live another time.

THOMAS CARLYLE

Lo, here hath been dawning another blue day;
Think, wilt thou let it slip useless away?

Out of eternity this new day is born,
Into eternity at night will return.

Behold it aforetime no eye ever did;
So soon it forever from all eyes is hid.

Here hath been dawning another blue day;
Think, wilt thou let it slip useless away?

KAHLIL GIBRAN

YOUR DAILY LIFE is your temple and your religion.

—◄《《◇《◇《《◇(◇)◇》◇》◇》◇—

from the writings of DALE CARNEGIE

I F YOU HAVE worries, there is no better way to eliminate them than by walking them off. Just take them out for a walk. They may take wings and fly away!

⊷§HENRY WADSWORTH LONGFELLOW

> Trust no future, howe'er pleasant!
> Let the dead past bury its dead!
> Act—act in the living Present!
> Heart within and God o'erhead.

⊷§EDWARD HOWARD GRIGGS

N O, THE RIVER of time sweeps on with regular, remorseless current. There are hours when we would give all we possess if we could but check the flow of its waters, there are other hours when we long to speed them more rapidly; but desire and effort alike are futile. Whether we work or sleep, are earnest or idle, rejoice or moan in agony, the river of time flows on with the same resistless flood; and it is only while the water of the river of time flows over the mill wheel of today's life that we can utilize it. Once it is past, it is in the great, unreturning sea of eternity. Other opportunities will come, other waters will flow; but that which has slipped by unused is lost utterly and will return not again.

❧BENJAMIN FRANKLIN

IF TIME BE of all things most precious, wasting time must be the greatest prodigality, since lost time is never found again; and what we call time enough always proves little enough. Let us then be up and doing, and doing to a purpose; so by diligence shall we do more with less perplexity.

❧WILLIAM ALLEN WHITE

I DO NOT fear tomorrow, for I have seen yesterday and I love today.

❧LORD CHESTERFIELD

I RECOMMEND YOU to take care of the minutes, for the hours will take care of themselves.

❧JOHN WANAMAKER

ONE MAY WALK over the highest mountain—one step at a time.

------------------◦◦◦◦◦◦(◦)◦◦◦◦◦------------------

from the writings of DALE CARNEGIE

REMEMBER THE NEXT time a cloud of unhappiness settles down on you, that you are merely not feeling equal to the tasks before you and that if you overcome this feeling your unhappiness very likely will disappear. Remember, too, that happiness comes and goes, like a revolving beacon light. It flashes brilliantly a moment, then it is gone. But if it shone all the time you wouldn't appreciate it.

from the writings of DALE CARNEGIE

IF YOU CAN'T sleep, then get up and do something instead of lying there and worrying. It's the worry that gets you, not the loss of sleep.

JEAN DE LA BRUYÈRE

CHILDREN HAVE NEITHER a past nor a future. Thus they enjoy the present—which seldom happens to us.

RALPH WALDO EMERSON

FINISH EACH DAY before you begin the next, and interpose a solid wall of sleep between the two. This you cannot do without temperance.

SENECA

SOME THERE ARE that torment themselves afresh with the memory of what is past; others, again, afflict themselves with the apprehension of evils to come; and very ridiculously both—for the one does not now concern us, and the other not yet. . . .

LORD CHESTERFIELD

KNOW THE TRUE value of time. Snatch, seize, and enjoy every moment of it. No idleness, no laziness, no procrastination. Never put off till tomorrow what you can do today.

—————————◦⟨◦⟨◦⟨◻⟩◦⟩◦⟩◦—————————

from the writings of DALE CARNEGIE

G IVE YOUR PROBLEM all the thought you possibly can
   before a solution is reached. But when the matter
is settled and over with, worry not at all.

———————————————————————————————

ᴇ§WILLIAM PENN

THERE IS NOTHING of which we are apt to be so lavish as of time,
and about which we ought to be more solicitous; since without it
we can do nothing in this world.

ᴇ§OMAR KHAYYÁM

   Tomorrow's fate, though thou be wise,
   Thou canst not tell nor yet surmise;
   Pass, therefore, not today in vain,
   For it will never come again.

ᴇ§THOMAS DREIER

IF WE ARE ever to enjoy life, now is the time—not tomorrow, nor
next year, nor in some future life after we have died. The best
preparation for a better life next year is a full, complete, harmonious,
joyous life this year. Our beliefs in a rich future life are of little
importance unless we coin them into a rich present life. Today
should always be our most wonderful day.

HENRY WADSWORTH LONGFELLOW

THE BUILDERS

All are architects of Fate,
　　Working in these walls of Time;
Some with massive deeds and great,
　　Some with ornaments of rhyme.

Nothing useless is, or low;
　　Each thing in its place is best;
And what seems but idle show
　　Strengthens and supports the rest.

For the structure that we raise,
　　Time is with materials filled;
Our todays and yesterdays
　　Are the blocks with which we build.

Truly shape and fashion these;
　　Leave no yawning gaps between.
Think not, because no man sees,
　　Such things will remain unseen.

In the elder days of Art,
　　Builders wrought with greatest care
Each minute and unseen part;
　　For the gods see everywhere.

Let us do our work as well,
　　Both the unseen and the seen;
Make the house, where gods may dwell,
　　Beautiful, entire, and clean.

Else our lives are incomplete,
  Standing in these walls of time,
Broken stairways, where the feet
  Stumble as they seek to climb.

Build today, then, strong and sure,
  With a firm and ample base;
And ascending and secure
  Shall tomorrow find its place.

Thus alone can we attain
  To those turrets, where the eye
Sees the world as one vast plain,
  And one boundless reach of sky.

ARNOLD BENNETT

TIME IS THE inexplicable raw material of everything. With it, all is possible; without it, nothing. The supply of time is truly a daily miracle, an affair genuinely astonishing when one examines it.

You wake up in the morning, and lo! your purse is magically filled with twenty-four hours of the unmanufactured tissue of the universe of your life! It is yours. It is the most precious of possessions. . . .

You have to live on this twenty-four hours of daily time. Out of it you have to spin health, pleasure, money, content, respect, and the evolution of your immortal soul. Its right use, its most effective use, is a matter of the highest urgency and of the most thrilling actuality. All depends on that. Your happiness . . . depends on that. . . .

We never shall have any more time. We have, and we have always had, all the time there is.

from the writings of DALE CARNEGIE

A S A CHILD I grew up on a Missouri farm; and one day, while helping my mother pit cherries, I began to cry. My mother said, "Dale, what in the world are you crying about?" I blubbered, "I'm afraid I am going to be buried alive!"

I was full of worries in those days. When thunderstorms came, I worried for fear I would be killed by lightning. When hard times came, I worried for fear we wouldn't have enough to eat. I worried for fear I would go to hell when I died. I was terrified for fear an older boy, Sam White, would cut off my big ears—as he threatened to do. I worried for fear girls would laugh at me if I tipped my hat to them. I worried for fear no girl would ever be willing to marry me. I worried about what I would say to my wife immediately after we were married. I imagined that we would be married in some country church, and then get in a surrey with fringe on the top and ride back to the farm . . . but how would I be able to keep the conversation going on that ride back to the farm? How? How? I pondered over that earthshaking problem for many an hour as I walked behind the plow.

As the years went by, I gradually discovered that 99 per cent of the things I worried about never happened.

↜JOHN MASON BROWN

SO OFTEN WE rob tomorrow's memories by today's economies.

↜BENJAMIN FRANKLIN

SINCE THOU ART not sure of a minute, throw not away an hour.

↜KALIDASA

Look to this day!
For it is life, the very life of life.
In its brief course
Lie all the verities and realities of your existence:
   The bliss of growth
   The glory of action
   The splendor of beauty,
For yesterday is but a dream
And tomorrow is only a vision,
But today well lived makes every yesterday a dream of happiness
And every tomorrow a vision of hope.
Look well, therefore, to this day!
Such is the salutation to the dawn.

↜PSALM 118

THIS IS THE day which the Lord hath made; we will rejoice and
be glad in it.

↜ANONYMOUS

IT'S BUT LITTLE good you'll do, watering last year's crops.

from the writings of DALE CARNEGIE

IF WE CAN'T have all we want, let's not poison our days with worry and resentment. Let's be good to ourselves. Let's be philosophical. And philosophy, according to Epictetus, boils down to this: "The essence of philosophy is that a man should so live that his happiness shall depend as little as possible on external things."

SIR WILLIAM OSLER

NOW EACH ONE of you is a much more marvelous organization than the great (ocean) liner, and bound on a longer voyage. What I urge is that you so learn to control the machinery as to live with "day-tight compartments" as the most certain way to ensure safety on the voyage. Get on the bridge, and see that at least the great bulkheads are in working order. Touch a button and hear, at every level of your life, the iron doors shutting out the Past—the dead yesterdays. Touch another and shut off, with a metal curtain, the Future—the unborn tomorrows. Then you are safe—safe for today! Shut off the past! Let the dead past bury its dead. . . . Shut out the yesterdays which have lighted fools the way to dusty death. . . . The load of tomorrow, added to that of yesterday, carried today, makes the strongest falter. Shut off the future as tightly as the past. . . . The future is today. . . . There is no tomorrow. . . . The day of man's salvation is now. Waste of energy, mental distress, nervous worries dog the steps of a man who is anxious about the future. . . . Shut close, then, the great fore and aft bulkheads, and prepare to cultivate the habit of a life of "day-tight compartments."

❧SENECA

WE ARE ALWAYS complaining that our days are few, and acting as though there would be no end to them.

❧GEORGE MACDONALD

THE BEST PREPARATION for the future is the present well seen to and the last duty done.

❧HENRY WADSWORTH LONGFELLOW

LOOK NOT MOURNFULLY to the past . . . it comes not back again; wisely improve the present—it is thine; go forth to meet the shadowy future without fear, and with a manly heart.

---

from the writings of DALE CARNEGIE

SUPPOSE WE ARE so discouraged that we feel there is no hope of our ever being able to turn our lemons into lemonade—then here are two reasons why we ought to try, anyway—two reasons why we have everything to gain and nothing to lose.

Reason one: We may succeed.

Reason two: Even if we don't succeed, the mere attempt to turn our minus into a plus will cause us to look forward instead of backward; it will replace negative thoughts with positive thoughts; it will release creative energy and spur us to get so busy that we won't have either the time or the inclination to mourn over what is past and forever gone.

from the writings of D A L E   C A R N E G I E

NO ONE LIVING has enough emotion and vigor to fight the inevitable and, at the same time, enough left over to create a new life. Choose one or the other. You can either bend with the inevitable sleet storms of life—or you can resist them and break.

I saw that happen on a farm in Missouri. I planted a score of trees on that farm. At first, they grew with astonishing rapidity. Then a sleet storm encrusted each twig and branch with a heavy coating of ice. Instead of bowing gracefully to their burden, these trees proudly resisted and broke and split under the load—and had to be destroyed. They hadn't learned the wisdom of the forests of the North. I have traveled hundreds of miles through the evergreen forests of Canada, yet I have never seen a spruce or a pine broken by sleet or ice. These evergreen forests know how to bend, how to bow down their branches, how to co-operate with the inevitable.

WILLIAM SHAKESPEARE

TAKE ALL THE swift advantage of the hours.

GEORGE WASHINGTON

WE OUGHT NOT to look back unless it is to derive useful lessons from past errors, and for the purpose of profiting by dear-bought experience.

from the writings of DALE CARNEGIE

HATE BURNS UP more energy than anything else, more than hard work, illness or justifiable worry. So when hatred is entering our hearts, let's just put it out, make room for pleasant thoughts instead, save our precious God-given energy for something worthy of it.

≈§SAMUEL JOHNSON

IT IS COMMON to overlook what is near by keeping the eye fixed on something remote. In the same manner present opportunities are neglected and attainable good is slighted by minds busied in extensive ranges, and intent upon future advantages. Life, however short, is made shorter by waste of time.

≈§RALPH WALDO EMERSON

FINISH EACH DAY and be done with it. . . . You have done what you could; some blunders and absurdities no doubt crept in; forget them as soon as you can. Tomorrow is a new day; you shall begin it well and serenely.

≈§JESUS

TAKE THEREFORE NO thought for the morrow; for the morrow shall take thought for the things of itself. Sufficient unto the day is the evil thereof.

≈ SYBYL F. PARTRIDGE

JUST FOR TODAY

J UST FOR TODAY I will be happy. This assumes what Abraham
Lincoln said is true, that "most folks are about as happy as they
make up their minds to be." Happiness is from within; it is not a
matter of externals.

Just for today I will try to adjust myself to what is, and not
try to adjust everything to my own desires. I will take my family,
my business, and my luck as they come and fit myself to them.

Just for today I will take care of my body. I will exercise it,
care for it, nourish it, not abuse it nor neglect it, so that it will be
a perfect machine for my bidding.

Just for today I will try to strengthen my mind. I will learn
something useful. I will not be a mental loafer. I will read something
that requires effort, thought and concentration.

Just for today I will exercise my soul in three ways. I will do
somebody a good turn and not get found out. I will do at least two
things I don't want to do, as William James suggests, just for
exercise.

Just for today I will be agreeable. I will look as well as I can,
dress as becomingly as possible, talk low, act courteously, be liberal
with praise, criticize not at all, nor find fault with anything and
not try to regulate nor improve anyone.

Just for today I will try to live through this day only, not to
tackle my whole life problem at once. I can do things for twelve
hours that would appall me if I had to keep them up for a lifetime.

Just for today I will have a program. I will write down what I
expect to do every hour. I may not follow it exactly, but I will have
it. I will eliminate two pests, hurry and indecision.

Just for today I will have a quiet half hour all by myself and relax. In this half hour sometimes I will think of God, so as to get a little more perspective into my life.

Just for today I will be unafraid, especially I will not be afraid to be happy, to enjoy what is beautiful, to love, and to believe that those I love, love me.

LIN YUTANG

THE SECRET OF contentment is knowing how to enjoy what you have, and to be able to lose all desire for things beyond your reach.

NORMAN VINCENT PEALE

ANY FACT FACING us is not as important as our attitude toward it, for that determines our success or failure. The way you think about a fact may defeat you before you ever do anything about it. You are overcome by the fact because you think you are.

HELEN KELLER

KEEP YOUR FACE to the sunshine and you cannot see the shadow.

MARY PICKFORD

TODAY IS A new day. You will get out of it just what you put into it. . . . If you have made mistakes, even serious mistakes, there is always another chance for you. And supposing you have tried and failed again and again, you may have a fresh start any moment you choose, for this thing that we call "failure" is not the falling down, but the staying down.

MADELINE S. BRIDGES

LIFE'S MIRROR

There are loyal hearts, there are spirits brave,
There are souls that are pure and true;
Then give to the world the best you have,
And the best will come back to you.

Give love, and love to your life will flow,
A strength in your utmost need;
Have faith, and a score of hearts will show
Their faith in your work and deed.

Give truth, and your gift will be paid in kind,
And honor will honor meet;
And the smile which is sweet will surely find
A smile that is just as sweet.

Give sorrow and pity to those who mourn;
You will gather in flowers again
The scattered seeds from your thought outborne
Though the sowing seemed but vain.

For life is the mirror of king and slave,
'Tis just what we are and do;
Then give to the world the best you have
And the best will come back to you.

from the writings of DALE CARNEGIE

REMEMBER HAPPINESS doesn't depend upon who you
are or what you have; it depends solely upon what
you think. So start each day by thinking of all the things
you have to be thankful for. Your future will depend
very largely on the thoughts you think today. So think
thoughts of hope and confidence and love and success.

ROBERT LOUIS STEVENSON

THE HABIT OF being happy enables one to be freed, or largely
freed, from the domination of outward conditions.

WILLIAM SHARP

IF YOU CANNOT be happy in one way, be in another; this facility
of disposition wants but little aid from philosophy, for health and
good humor are almost the whole affair. Many run about after
felicity, like an absent-minded man hunting for his hat, while it is
in his hand or on his head.

FRANÇOIS DE LA ROCHEFOUCAULD

HAPPINESS IS IN the taste, and not in the things themselves. It is
by having what we like that we are made happy, not by having
what others think desirable.

⊷WILHELM VON HUMBOLDT

I AM MORE and more convinced that our happiness or unhappiness depends far more on the way we meet the events of life than on the nature of those events themselves.

⊷JAMES OPPENHEIM

THE FOOLISH MAN seeks happiness in the distance; the wise grows it under his feet.

---

from the writings of DALE CARNEGIE

WE ALL GET breaks every month in the year, but we recognize few of them if we aren't prepared. Watch for your break this month.

⊷CHARLES H. SPURGEON

IT IS NOT how much we have, but how much we enjoy, that makes happiness.

⊷RALPH WALDO EMERSON

THIS TIME, LIKE all times, is a very good one, if we but know what to do with it.

⊷FRANÇOIS DE LA ROCHEFOUCAULD

THE HAPPINESS OR unhappiness of men depends no less upon their dispositions than on their fortunes.

from the writings of DALE CARNEGIE

THE MAN WHO grasps an opportunity as it is paraded before him, nine times out of ten makes a success; but the man who makes his own opportunities is, barring an accident, a sure-fire success!

◄§ JOSEPH ADDISON

CHEERFULNESS KEEPS UP a kind of daylight in the mind, and fills it with a steady and perpetual serenity.

◄§ TERENCE

LIFE IS LIKE a game of tables; the chances are not in our power, but the playing is.

◄§ FRANCIS BACON

IT CANNOT BE denied that outward accidents conduce much to fortune; favor, opportunity, death of others, occasion fitting virtue; but chiefly, the mold of a man's fortune is in his own hands.

◄§ ROBERT HERRICK

Learn this of me, where e'r thy lot doth fall;
Short lot, or not, to be content with all.

◄§ *THE TATLER*

EVERY MAN IS the maker of his own fortune.

from the writings of DALE CARNEGIE

IT ISN'T WHAT you have or who you are or where you are or what you are doing that makes you happy or unhappy. It is what you think about it. For example, two people may be in the same place, doing the same thing; both may have about an equal amount of money and prestige—and yet one may be miserable and the other happy. Why? Because of different mental attitude.

⋑ JOHN DRYDEN

IT IS A madness to make fortune the mistress of events, because in herself she is nothing, but is ruled by prudence.

⋑ DEAN WILLIAM R. INGE

WE MUST CUT our coat according to our cloth, and adapt ourselves to changing circumstances.

⋑ BENJAMIN DISRAELI

NEXT TO KNOWING when to seize an opportunity, the most important thing in life is to know when to forego an advantage.

⋑ LOGAN PEARSALL SMITH

THERE ARE TWO things to aim at in life: first, to get what you want; and after that, to enjoy it. Only the wisest of mankind achieve the second.

&FRIEDRICH NIETZSCHE

WHEN ONE HAS much to put into them, a day has a hundred pockets.

&GILBERT KEITH CHESTERTON

TRUE CONTENTMENT IS the power of getting out of any situation all that there is in it.

&ROBERT LOUIS STEVENSON

THERE IS NO duty we so much underrate as the duty of being happy.

&MARK TWAIN

HAPPINESS IS A Swedish sunset—it is there for all, but most of us look the other way and lose it.

&LEO TOLSTOI

MAN IS MEANT for happiness and this happiness is in him, in the satisfaction of the daily needs of his existence.

---

from the writings of DALE CARNEGIE

MANY PEOPLE THINK that if they were only in some other place, or had some other job, they would be happy. Well, that is doubtful. So get as much happiness out of what you are doing as you can and don't put off being happy until some future date.

❧ELLA WHEELER WILCOX

> Our lives are songs; God writes the
> words
> And we set them to music at
> pleasure;
> And the song grows glad, or sweet
> or sad,
> As we choose to fashion the measure.

❧ANONYMOUS

IF YOU WANT to sing, you will find a song.

❧GEORGE SAND

ONE IS HAPPY as a result of one's own efforts, once one knows the necessary ingredients of happiness—simple tastes, a certain degree of courage, self-denial to a point, love of work, and, above all, a clear conscience. Happiness is no vague dream, of that I now feel certain. By the proper use of experience and thought one can draw much from oneself, by determination and patience one can even restore one's health—so let us live life as it is, and not be ungrateful.

***

from the writings of DALE CARNEGIE

LIFE TRULY IS a boomerang. What you give, you get.

from the writings of DALE CARNEGIE

I KNOW MEN AND women can banish worry, fear and various kinds of illnesses, and can transform their lives by changing their thoughts. I know! I know! I know! I have seen such incredible transformations performed hundreds of times. I have seen them so often that I no longer wonder at them.

JOHANN WOLFGANG VON GOETHE

HE WHO ENJOYS doing and enjoys what he has done is happy.

LAURENCE STERNE

WHAT A LARGE volume of adventures may be grasped within the little span of life, by him who interests his heart in everything, and who, having eyes to see what time and chance are perpetually holding out to him as he journeyeth on his way, misses nothing he can fairly lay his hands on!

MARCUS AURELIUS

ADAPT YOURSELF TO the things among which your lot has been cast and love sincerely the fellow creatures with whom destiny has ordained that you shall live.

HENRY S. HASKINS

ALMOST ANY EVENT will put on a new face when received with cheerful acceptance and no questions asked.

from the writings of DALE CARNEGIE

THE CHIEF THING you are seeking in this world is happiness; and happiness does not depend upon good health or money or fame, though good health is a large factor. It depends, however, principally on one thing only: your thoughts. If you can't have what you want, be grateful for what you have. Keep thinking constantly of all the big things you have to be thankful for instead of complaining about the little things that annoy you.

GILBERT KEITH CHESTERTON

THE TRUEST KINSHIP with humanity would lie in doing as humanity has always done, accepting with sportsmanlike relish the estate to which we are called, the star of our happiness, and the fortunes of the land of our birth.

CHARLES BAUDELAIRE

HE WHO DOESN'T accept the conditions of life sells his soul.

BERTRAND RUSSELL

THE SECRET OF happiness is this: Let your interests be as wide as possible, and let your reactions to the things and persons that interest you be as far as possible friendly rather than hostile.

◆§ JOHN MILTON

THE MIND IS its own place, and in itself can make a heaven of Hell, a hell of Heaven.

◆§ MICHEL EYQUEM DE MONTAIGNE

A MAN IS not hurt so much by what happens, as by his opinion of what happens.

---

from the writings of DALE CARNEGIE

I KNOW WITH A conviction beyond all doubt that the biggest problem you and I have to deal with—in fact, almost the only problem we have to deal with—is choosing the right thoughts. If we can do that, we will be on the highroad to solving all our problems.

◆§ JOHN RUSKIN

ALL REAL AND wholesome enjoyments possible to man have been just as possible to him since first he was made of the earth as they are now; and they are possible to him chiefly in peace. To watch the corn grow, and the blossoms set; to draw hard breath over plowshare or spade; to read, to think, to love, to hope, to pray— these are the things that make men happy. . . . Now and then a wearied king, or a tormented slave, found out where the true kingdoms of the world were, and possessed himself, in a furrow or two of garden ground, of a truly infinite dominion.

from the writings of DALE CARNEGIE

A M I ADVOCATING that we simply bow down to all the adversities that come our way? Not by a long shot! That is mere fatalism. As long as there is a chance that we can save a situation, let's fight! But when common sense tells us that we are up against something that is so—and cannot be otherwise—then, in the name of our sanity, let's not "look before and after and pine for what is not."

JAMES M. BARRIE

THE SECRET OF happiness is not in doing what one likes, but in liking what one has to do.

HONORÉ DE BALZAC

WE EXAGGERATE MISFORTUNE and happiness alike. We are never either so wretched or so happy as we say we are.

EDWIN MARKHAM

PREPAREDNESS

For all your days prepare,
And meet them ever alike:
When you are the anvil, bear—
When you are the hammer, strike.

SAMUEL JOHNSON

TO IMPROVE THE golden moment of opportunity, and catch the good that is within our reach, is the great art of life.

EDWARD EVERETT HALE

> To look up and not down,
> To look forward and not back,
> To look out and not in, and
> To lend a hand.

------

from the writings of DALE CARNEGIE

OBVIOUSLY, CIRCUMSTANCES alone do not make us happy or unhappy. It is the way we react to circumstances that determines our feeling. Jesus said that the kingdom of heaven is within you. That is where the kingdom of hell is too.

CHARLES KINGSLEY

THE MEN WHOM I have seen succeed best in life have always been cheerful and hopeful men, who went about their business with a smile on their faces, and took the changes and chances of this mortal life like men, facing rough and smooth alike as it came.

EDGAR W. HOWE

EVERY SUCCESSFUL MAN I have heard of has done the best he could with conditions as he found them, and not waited until next year for better.

from the writings of DALE CARNEGIE

As you and I march across the decades of time, we are going to meet a lot of unpleasant situations that are so. They cannot be otherwise. We have our choice. We can either accept them as inevitable and adjust ourselves to them, or we can ruin our lives with rebellion and maybe end up with a nervous breakdown.

SIR WILLIAM OSLER

THINGS CANNOT ALWAYS go your way. Learn to accept in silence the minor aggravations, cultivate the gift of taciturnity and consume your own smoke with an extra draught of hard work, so that those about you may not be annoyed with the dust and soot of your complaints.

JOHN BURROUGHS

THE LURE OF the distant and the difficult is deceptive. The great opportunity is where you are.

SAMUEL BUTLER

ALL OF THE animals except man know that the principal business of life is to enjoy it.

EPICTETUS

HE IS A wise man who does not grieve for the things which he has not, but rejoices for those which he has.

⁓ MARCUS AURELIUS

LET NOT YOUR mind run on what you lack as much as on what you have already. Of the things you have, select the best; and then reflect how eagerly they would have been sought if you did not have them.

⁓ WILLIAM JAMES

ACTION SEEMS TO follow feeling, but really action and feeling go together; and by regulating the action, which is under the more direct control of the will, we can indirectly regulate the feeling, which is not.

Thus the sovereign voluntary path to cheerfulness, if our cheerfulness be lost, is to sit up cheerfully and to act and speak as if cheerfulness were already there.

⁓ FREDERICK LANGBRIDGE

Two men look out through the same
    bars;
One sees the mud, and one the stars. . . .

---

from the writings of DALE CARNEGIE

THE TROUBLE WITH most of us is that we keep our eyes closed to opportunities that thrust themselves at us; and rare is the man who searches for his opportunity or sees one even when he stumbles over it.

━━━━━━◆《◆《◆(O)◆》◆》◆━━━━━━

from the writings of DALE CARNEGIE

WHEN ILL LUCK besets us, to ease the tension we have only to remember that happiness is relative. The next time you are tempted to grumble about what has happened to you, why not pause and be glad that it is no worse than it is.

WILLIAM JAMES

MUCH OF WHAT we call evil . . . can often be converted into a bracing and tonic good by a simple change of the sufferer's inner attitude from one of fear to one of fight.

SAMUEL JOHNSON

THE HABIT OF looking on the best side of every event is worth more than a thousand pounds a year.

JULIUS ROSENWALD

WHEN YOU HAVE a lemon, make a lemonade.

VICTORIA SACKVILLE-WEST

HOW VERY INGENIOUS some people are at making the most of a meager opportunity! It bears out my contention that, other things being equal, people's success usually lies in their own hands. A bit of extra enterprise and imagination can lift their ideas right out of the conventional without involving a lot of labor or expense. . . . There is scope for inventiveness everywhere if only we have the vision to perceive it. The breakers-away are the creators.

WILLIAM JAMES

BE WILLING TO have it so. Acceptance of what has happened is the first step in overcoming the consequences of any misfortune.

LIN YUTANG

TRUE PEACE OF mind comes from accepting the worst. Psychologically, I think, it means a release of energy.

ALBERT SCHWEITZER

MAN MUST CEASE attributing his problems to his environment, and learn again to exercise his will—his personal responsibility in the realm of faith and morals.

EPICTETUS

AT EVERY OCCASION in your life, do not forget to commune with yourself and to ask of yourself how you can profit by it.

---

from the writings of DALE CARNEGIE

HERE'S A THOUGHT to carry with us: Let's forget everything that arouses rancor, distrust and unkindness in our minds. At any time you can adopt the practice of forgetting a wrong. How? By not letting thoughts of it creep into your mind. If you think only kind, generous, happy and helpful thoughts, rancor can't possibly have any place in your mind, and your life will be filled with contentment.

from the writings of DALE CARNEGIE

IF WE THINK happy thoughts, we will be happy. If we think miserable thoughts, we will be miserable. If we think fear thoughts, we will be fearful. If we think sickly thoughts, we will probably be ill. If we think failure, we will certainly fail. If we wallow in self-pity, everyone will want to shun us and avoid us.

GEORGE BERNARD SHAW

PEOPLE ARE ALWAYS blaming their circumstances for what they are. I don't believe in circumstances. The people who get on in this world are the people who get up and look for the circumstances they want, and, if they can't find them, make them.

ROBERT SOUTHWELL

My conscience is my crown,
Contented thoughts my rest;
My heart is happy in itself;
My bliss is in my breast.

LORD HOUGHTON

A MAN'S BEST things are nearest him, lie close about his feet.

ABRAHAM LINCOLN

I'LL STUDY AND get ready and be prepared for my opportunity when it comes.

❧MARCUS AURELIUS

OUR LIFE IS what our thoughts make it.

❧WILLIAM JAMES

NO MATTER HOW full a reservoir of maxims one may possess, and no matter how good one's sentiments may be, if one has not taken advantage of every concrete opportunity to act, one's character may remain entirely unaffected for the better. With mere good intentions, hell is proverbially paved.

❧JOSIAH G. HOLLAND

IT IS NOT a question of how much a man knows, but of the use he makes of what he knows; not a question of what he has acquired, and how he has been trained, but of what he is and what he can do.

---

from the writings of DALE CARNEGIE

DO YOU KNOW that if you are courteous and pleasant all day during your work that you will go home at night less fatigued than if you gave way to irritation? Pleasantry, light laughs, relieve tension. It isn't work that makes you tired, it's your mental attitude. Try it.

❧FREDERICK W. ROBERTSON

IT IS NOT the situation that makes the man, but the man who makes the situation. The slave may be a freeman. The monarch may be slave. Situations are noble or ignoble, as we make them.

from the writings of DALE CARNEGIE

Do YOU KNOW that you can be happy by just making up your mind—and sticking to it—that you are going to be happy? Happiness depends upon your state of mind, not upon your possessions or your achievement. First, you must insist upon creating your own philosophy of life. Don't let what another says or does affect you to the degree that he or she is influencing your beliefs.

Second, when you are feeling unhappy, take a walk on a beautiful day, to some beautiful spot. Think of the loveliness around you. If you do this, you cannot be wholly unhappy at the moment. And that moment may set your pattern for the day, or the week, or the month, or for life.

Third, read a beautiful poem, listen to beautiful music.

Fourth (and this will be one of the most potent influences), do a kind deed for someone else.

Fifth, if you are a woman, see that your house is in order, add to its tidiness and beauty.

Sixth, keep as healthy as possible. You don't have to let develop such ailments as the various forms of rheumatism, arthritis, neuritis, high blood pressure and others that can become chronic. If you do, you are being careless with yourself.

Seventh, get a hobby. Make that hobby something you have always been interested in.

from the writings of DALE CARNEGIE

BY TALKING TO yourself every hour of the day, you can direct yourself to think thoughts of courage and happiness, thoughts of power and peace. By talking to yourself about the things you have to be grateful for, you can fill your mind with thoughts that soar and sing.

SAINT BERNARD

NOTHING CAN WORK me damage except myself. The harm that I sustain I carry about with me, and am never a real sufferer but by my own fault.

WILLIAM WARE

THE SHAPING OF our own life is our own work. It is a thing of beauty, or a thing of shame, as we ourselves make it. We lay the corner and add joint to joint, we give the proportion, we set the finish. It may be a thing of beauty and of joy forever. God forgive us if we pervert our life from putting on its appointed glory!

GEORGE ELIOT

WHAT IS OPPORTUNITY to the man who can't use it? An unfecundated egg, which the waves of time wash away into nonentity.

FRANCIS BACON

A WISE MAN will make more opportunities than he finds.

from the writings of DALE CARNEGIE

IS GIVING YOURSELF a pep talk every day silly, super-
ficial, childish? No. On the contrary, it is the very
essence of sound psychology. "Our life is what our
thoughts make it." Those words are just as true today
as they were eighteen centuries ago when Marcus Aurelius
first wrote them in his book of *Meditations*.

EDMUND SPENSER

IT IS THE mind that maketh good or ill, that maketh wretch or
happy, rich or poor.

LAURENCE STERNE

I PITY THE man who can travel from Dan to Beersheba, and cry,
'tis all barren—and so it is, and so is all the world to him who will
not cultivate the fruits it offers.

JOHN FOSTER

AN OBSERVANT MAN, in all his intercourse with society and the
world, constantly and unperceived marks on every person and thing
the figure expressive of its value, and therefore, on meeting that
person or thing, knows instantly what kind and degree of attention
to give it. This is to make something of experience.

BENJAMIN DISRAELI

THE SECRET OF success in life is for a man to be ready for his
opportunity when it comes.

❧HELEN KELLER

THE MILLION LITTLE things that drop into our hands, the small opportunities each day brings, He leaves us free to use or abuse and goes unchanging along His silent way.

❧SIR JOHN LUBBOCK

EVERYONE MUST HAVE felt that a cheerful friend is like a sunny day, which sheds its brightness on all around; and most of us can, as we choose, make of this world either a palace or a prison.

❧CHARLES BUXTON

YOU WILL NEVER "find" time for anything. If you want time you must make it.

❧THOMAS JONES

MANY DO WITH opportunities as children do at the seashore; they fill their little hands with sand, and then let the grains fall through, one by one, till all are gone.

---

from the writings of DALE CARNEGIE

THERE IS ONLY one way on God's green footstool that the past can be constructive; and that is by calmly analyzing our past mistakes and profiting by them—and forgetting them.

ᵉᣬHELEN KELLER

I BELIEVE THAT we can live on earth according to the teachings of Jesus, and that the greatest happiness will come to the world when man obeys His commandment that "ye love one another."

I believe that every question between man and man is a religious question, and that every social wrong is a moral wrong.

I believe that we can live on earth according to the fulfillment of God's will, and that when the will of God is done on earth as it is in heaven, every man will love his fellow men and act toward them as he desires they should act toward him. I believe that the welfare of each is bound up in the welfare of all.

I believe that life is given us so we may grow in love, and I believe that God is in me as the sun is in the color and fragrance of a flower—the Light in my darkness, the Voice in my silence.

I believe that only in broken gleams has the Sun of Truth yet shone upon men. I believe that love will finally establish the Kingdom of God on earth, and that the cornerstones of that Kingdom will be Liberty, Truth, Brotherhood and Service.

I believe that no good shall be lost, and that all man has willed or hoped or dreamed of good shall exist forever.

I believe in the immortality of the soul because I have within me immortal longings. I believe that the state we enter after death is wrought of our own motives, thoughts and deeds. I believe that in the life to come I shall have the senses I have not had here, and that my home there will be beautiful with color, music, and speech of flowers and faces I love.

Without this faith there would be little meaning in my life. I should be "a mere pillar of darkness in the dark." Observers in the full enjoyment of their bodily senses pity me, but it is because they do not see the golden chamber in my life where I dwell delighted; for, dark as my path may seem to them, I carry a magic light in my heart. Faith, the spiritual strong searchlight, illumines the way, and although sinister doubts lurk in the shadow, I walk unafraid toward the Enchanted Wood where the foliage is always green, where joy abides, where nightingales nest and sing, and where life and death are one in the Presence of the Lord.

WILLIAM SHAKESPEARE

My crown is in my heart, not on my head;
Not deck'd with diamonds and Indian stones,
Nor to be seen: my crown is called content;
A crown it is that seldom kings enjoy.

MAHATMA GANDHI

PRAYER IS THE very soul and essence of religion and therefore prayer must be the very core of the life of man, for no man can live without religion.

CARDINAL FRANCIS J. SPELLMAN

PRAY AS IF everything depended on God, and work as if everything depended upon man.

MARTIN LUTHER

A mighty fortress is our God,
A bulwark never failing,
Our helper he amid the flood
Of mortal ills prevailing.

from the writings of DALE CARNEGIE

YOU WILL RECALL that the White Queen said: "The rule is jam tomorrow and jam yesterday but never jam today." Most of us are like that—stewing about yesterday's jam and worrying about tomorrow's jam— instead of spreading today's jam thick on our bread right now.

JOHN JAY

GOD IS GREAT, and therefore he will be sought: he is good, and therefore he will be found.

If in the day of sorrow we own God's presence in the cloud, we shall find him also in the pillar of fire, brightening and cheering our way as the night comes on.

In all his dispensations God is at work for our good. In prosperity he tries our gratitude; in mediocrity, our contentment; in misfortune, our submission; in darkness, our faith; under temptation, our steadfastness; and at all times, our obedience and trust in him.

God governs the world, and we have only to do our duty wisely, and leave the issue to him.

VICTOR HUGO

CERTAIN THOUGHTS ARE prayers. There are moments when, whatever be the attitude of the body, the soul is on its knees.

JOHN BURROUGHS

ONE OF THE hardest lessons we have to learn in this life, and one that many persons never learn, is to see the divine, the celestial, the pure in the common, the near at hand—to see that heaven lies about us here in this world.

SÖREN KIERKEGAARD

PRAYER DOES NOT change God, but changes him who prays.

---

from the writings of DALE CARNEGIE

ONE OF THE most tragic things I know about human nature is that all of us tend to put off living. We are all dreaming of some magical rose garden over the horizon —instead of enjoying the roses that are blooming outside our windows today.

GEORGE MACDONALD

> A voice in the wind I do not know;
> A meaning on the face of the high hills
> Whose utterance I cannot comprehend.
> A something is behind them: that is God.

JOHANN WOLFGANG VON GOETHE

FAITH IS HIDDEN household capital.

✍HANS CHRISTIAN ANDERSEN

EVERY MAN'S LIFE is a fairy tale written by God's fingers.

✍JOSEPH ADDISON

THE PERSON WHO has a firm trust in the Supreme Being is powerful in His power, wise by His wisdom, happy by His happiness.

✍SAINT AUGUSTINE

FAITH IS TO believe what we do not see; and the reward of this faith is to see what we believe.

✍PLATO

WE ARE TWICE armed if we fight with faith.

---

from the writings of DALE CARNEGIE

YOU AND I are standing this very second at the meeting place of two eternities: the vast past that has endured forever, and the future that is plunging on to the last syllable of recorded time. We can't possibly live in either of those eternities—no, not even for one split second. But, by trying to do so, we can wreck both our bodies and our minds. So let's be content to live the only time we can possibly live: from now until bedtime.

from the writings of DALE CARNEGIE

O NE OF THE most appalling comments on our present way of life is that half of all the beds in our hospitals are reserved for patients with nervous and mental troubles, patients who have collapsed under the crushing burden of accumulated yesterdays and fearful tomorrows. Yet a vast majority of those people would be walking the streets today, leading happy, useful lives, if they had only heeded the words of Jesus: "Have no anxiety about the morrow"; or the words of Sir William Osler: "Live in day-tight compartments."

SAMUEL TAYLOR COLERIDGE

He prayeth best who loveth best
All things both great and small;
For the dear God who loveth us,
He made and loveth all.

IZAAK WALTON

WHEN I WOULD beget content and increase confidence in the power and wisdom and providence of Almighty God, I will walk the meadows by some gliding stream, and there contemplate the lilies that take no care, and those very many other little living creatures that are not only created, but fed (man knows not how) by the goodness of the God of Nature, and therefore trust in Him.

from the writings of DALE CARNEGIE

BY ALL MEANS take thought for the morrow, yes, careful thought and planning and preparation. But have no anxiety.

JOHN HENRY NEWMAN

 Lead, kindly Light, amid the encircling gloom,
 Lead Thou me on!
 The night is dark, and I am far from home—
 Lead Thou me on!
 Keep Thou my feet; I do not ask to see
 The distant scene—one step enough for me.

 I was not ever thus, nor prayed that Thou
 Shouldst lead me on.
 I loved to choose and see my path; but now
 Lead Thou me on!
 I loved the garish day, and, spite of fears,
 Pride ruled my will: Remember not past years.

 So long Thy power has blest me, sure it still
 Will lead me on
 O'er moor and fen, o'er crag and torrent, till
 The night is gone;
 And with the morn those angel faces smile
 Which I have loved long since, and lost awhile!

✑§HELEN KELLER

IT NEED NOT discourage us if we are full of doubts. Healthy questions keep faith dynamic. In fact, unless we start with doubts we cannot have a deep-rooted faith. One who believes lightly and unthinkingly has not much of a belief. He who has a faith which is not to be shaken has won it through blood and tears—has worked his way from doubt to truth as one who reaches a clearing through a thicket of brambles and thorns.

---

from the writings of DALE CARNEGIE

TODAY IS LIFE—the only life you are sure of. Make the most of today. Get interested in something. Shake yourself awake. Develop a hobby. Let the winds of enthusiasm sweep through you. Live today with gusto.

✑§GEORGE DAVID STEWART

TIME SPENT ON the knees in prayer will do more to remedy heart strain and nerve worry than anything else.

✑§JACK DEMPSEY

I NEVER WENT to bed in my life and I never ate a meal in my life without saying a prayer. I know my prayers have been answered thousands of times, and I know that I never said a prayer in my life without something good coming of it.

WILLIAM BLAKE

> To see a world in a grain of sand,
> And heaven in a wild flower,
> Hold infinity in the palm of your hand,
> And eternity in an hour.

MATTHEW 7:7

ASK, AND IT shall be given you; seek, and ye shall find; knock, and it shall be opened unto you.

ABRAHAM LINCOLN

I TOLD GOD that I had done all that I could and that now the result was in His hands; that if this country was to be saved, it was because He so willed it! The burden rolled off my shoulders. My intense anxiety was relieved and in its place came a great trustfulness!

MARTIN LUTHER

ALL WHO CALL on God in true faith, earnestly from the heart, will certainly be heard, and will receive what they have asked and desired.

HELEN KELLER

OFTEN WHEN THE heart is torn with sorrow, spiritually we wander like a traveler lost in a deep wood. We grow frightened, lose all sense of direction, batter ourselves against trees and rocks in our attempt to find a path. All the while there is a path—the path of Faith—that leads straight out of the dense tangle of our difficulties into the open road we are seeking.

from the writings of DALE CARNEGIE

THIS DAY IS too precious to be corroded by acid worries and vitriolic regrets. Keep your chin high and your thoughts sparkling, a mountain brook leaping in the spring sunshine. Seize this day. It will never come again.

ALFRED, LORD TENNYSON

More things are wrought by prayer
Than this world dreams of. Wherefore, let thy voice
Rise like a fountain for me night and day.
For what are men better than sheep or goats
That nourish a blind life within the brain,
If, knowing God, they lift not hands of prayer
Both for themselves and those who call them friend?
For so the whole round earth is every way
Bound by gold chains about the feet of God.

BENJAMIN FRANKLIN

AND HAVE WE now forgotten that powerful Friend? Or do we imagine we no longer need His assistance? I have lived a long time; and the longer I live, the move convincing proofs I see of this truth: that God governs in the affairs of men. And if a sparrow cannot fall to the ground without His notice, is it probable that an empire can rise without His aid?

JAMES A. GARFIELD

THERE ARE TWO people I must please—God and Garfield. I must live with Garfield here, with God hereafter.

HELEN KELLER

A SIMPLE, CHILDLIKE faith in a Divine Friend solves all the problems that come to us by land or sea. Difficulties meet us at every turn. They are the accompaniment of life. They result from combinations of character and individual idiosyncrasies. The surest way to meet them is to assume that we are immortal and that we have a Friend who "slumbers not, nor sleeps," and who watches over us and guides us—if we but let Him. With this thought strongly entrenched in our inmost being, we can do almost anything we wish and need not limit the things we think. We may help ourselves to all the beauty of the universe that we can hold. For every hurt there is recompense of tender sympathy. Out of pain grow the violets of patience and sweetness, the vision of the Holy Fire that touched the lips of Isaiah and kindled his life into spirit, and the contentment that comes with the evening star. The marvelous richness of human experience would lose something of rewarding joy if there were no limitations to overcome. The hilltop hour would not be half so wonderful if there were no dark valley to traverse.

ROBERT BROWNING

The year's at the spring,
And the day's at the morn;
Morning's at seven;
The hillside's dew-pearled;
The lark's on the wing;
The snail's on the thorn;
God's in His heaven—
All's right with the world!

from the writings of DALE CARNEGIE

STRANGE THAT WE so seldom recognize happiness until it has passed, that we rarely recognize it when it is on our doorstep.

HENRY FORD

I BELIEVE GOD is managing affairs and that He doesn't need any advice from me. With God in charge, I believe everything will work out for the best in the end. So what is there to worry about?

WILLIAM JAMES

THE TURBULENT BILLOWS of the fretful surface leave the deep parts of the ocean undisturbed; and to him who has a hold on vaster and more permanent realities, the hourly vicissitudes of his personal destiny seem relatively insignificant things. The really religious person is accordingly unshakable and full of equanimity and calmly ready for any duty that the day may bring forth.

FRANCIS BACON

A LITTLE PHILOSOPHY inclineth man's mind to atheism; but depth in philosophy bringeth men's minds about to religion.

WILLIAM JAMES

FAITH IS ONE of the forces by which men live, and the total absence of it means collapse.

from the writings of DALE CARNEGIE

ONE SURE WAY to forgive and forget our enemies is to become absorbed in some cause infinitely bigger than ourselves. Then the insults and enmities we encounter won't matter because we will be oblivious of everything but our cause.

WALT WHITMAN

I find letters from God dropped in the street, and every one is signed by God's name.

And I leave them where they are, for I know that whereso'er I go,

Others will punctually come for ever and ever.

CARL JUNG

DURING THE PAST thirty years, people from all the civilized countries of the earth have consulted me. Many hundreds of patients have passed through my hands. . . . Among all my patients in the second half of life—that is to say, over thirty-five—there has not been one whose problem in the last resort was not that of finding a religious outlook on life. It is safe to say that every one of them fell ill because he had lost what the living religions of every age have given to their followers, and none of them has been really healed who did not regain his religious outlook.

◄§EMILY DICKINSON

CHARTLESS

I never saw a moor,
I never saw the sea;
Yet know I how the heather looks,
And what a wave must be.

I never spoke with God,
Nor visited in heaven;
Yet certain am I of the spot
As if the chart were given.

◄§HELEN KELLER

I TRUST, AND nothing that happens disturbs my trust. I recognize
the beneficence of the power which we all worship as supreme—
Order, Fate, the Great Spirit, Nature, God. I recognize this power
in the sun that makes all things grow and keeps life afoot. I make a
friend of this indefinable force, and straightway I feel glad, brave
and ready for any lot Heaven may decree for me. This is my religion
of optimism.

◄§MAHATMA GANDHI

WITHOUT PRAYER I should have been a lunatic long ago.

◄§RICHARD E. BYRD

THE HUMAN RACE is not alone in the universe. . . . I am not alone.

⮜ＰＳＡＬＭ 121

I WILL LIFT up mine eyes unto the hills, from whence cometh my help.

My help cometh from the Lord, which made heaven and earth.

He will not suffer thy foot to be moved: he that keepeth thee will not slumber.

Behold, he that keepeth Israel shall neither slumber nor sleep.

The Lord is thy keeper: the Lord is thy shade upon thy right hand.

The sun shall not smite thee by day, nor the moon by night.

The Lord shall preserve thee from all evil: he shall preserve thy soul.

The Lord shall preserve thy going out and thy coming in from this time forth, and even for evermore.

⮜ＷＩＬＬＩＡＭ ＪＡＭＥＳ

PRAYER IS RELIGION in act; that is, prayer is real religion. It is prayer that distinguishes the religious phenomenon from such similar or neighboring phenomena as purely moral or esthetic sentiment. Religion is nothing if it be not the vital act by which the entire mind seeks to save itself by clinging to the principle from which it draws its life. This act is prayer, by which term I understand no vain exercise of words, no mere repetition of certain sacred formulae, but the very movement itself of the soul, putting itself in a personal relation of contact with the mysterious power—of which it feels the presence—it may be even before it has a name by which to call it. Whenever this interior prayer is lacking, there is no religion; wherever, on the other hand, this rises and stirs the soul, even in the absence of forms and doctrines, we have living religion.

⋖⋘⋖⋘⋖(⫶)⋗⋙⋗⋙⋗

from the writings of DALE CARNEGIE

THE FACT THAT we don't understand the mysteries of our bodies or electricity or a gas engine doesn't keep us from using or enjoying them. The fact that I don't understand the mysteries of prayer and religion no longer keeps me from enjoying the richer, happier life that religion brings. At long last, I realize the wisdom of Santayana's words: "Man is not made to understand life, but to live it."

I have gone back—well, I was about to say that I had gone back to religion; but that would not be accurate. I have gone forward to a new concept of religion. I no longer have the faintest interest in the differences in creeds that divide the churches. But I am tremendously interested in what religion does for me, just as I am interested in what electricity and good food and water do for me. They help me to lead a richer, fuller, happier life. But religion does far more than that. It brings me spiritual values. It gives me, as William James put it, "a new zest for life . . . more life, a larger, richer, more satisfying life." It gives me faith, hope and courage. It banishes tensions, anxieties, fears and worries. It gives purpose to my life—and direction. It vastly improves my happiness. It gives me abounding health. It helps me to create for myself "an oasis of peace amidst the whirling sands of life."

HARRY EMERSON FOSDICK

GOD IS NOT a cosmic bellboy for whom we can press a button to get things done.

DR. ALEXIS CARREL

PRAYER IS THE most powerful form of energy one can generate. It is a force as real as terrestrial gravity. As a physician, I have seen men, after all other therapy had failed, lifted out of disease and melancholy by the serene effort of prayer. . . . Prayer like radium is a source of luminous, self-generating energy. . . . In prayer, human beings seek to augment their finite energy by addressing themselves to the Infinite source of all energy. When we pray, we link ourselves with the inexhaustible motive power that spins the universe. We ask that a part of this power be apportioned to our needs. Even in asking, our human deficiencies are filled and we arise strengthened and repaired. . . . Whenever we address God in fervent prayer, we change both soul and body for the better. It could not happen that any man or woman could pray for a single moment without some good result.

JOHN GREENLEAF WHITTIER

> I know not where His islands lift
> Their fronded palms in air;
> I only know I cannot drift
> Beyond His love and care.

TRYON EDWARDS

ANXIETY IS THE rust of life, destroying its brightness and weakening its power. A childlike and abiding trust in Providence is its best preventive and remedy.

from the writings of DALE CARNEGIE

WHEN WE ARE harassed and reach the limit of our own strength, many of us then turn in desperation to God—"There are no atheists in foxholes." But why wait till we are desperate? Why not renew our strength every day? Why wait even until Sunday? For years I have had the habit of dropping into empty churches on weekday afternoons.

CHARLES WESLEY

I know that my Redeemer lives,
   And ever prays for me;
A token of His love He gives,
   A pledge of liberty.

I find Him lifting up my head;
   He brings salvation near;
His presence makes me free indeed,
   And He will soon appear.

He wills that I should holy be;
   What can withstand His will?
The counsel of His grace in me
   He surely shall fulfill.

When God is mine, and I am His,
   Of paradise possessed,
I taste unutterable bliss,
   And everlasting rest.

3

How to Win Friends and Influ-ence People is a book on human rela-tions—on getting along with people, on the need for friends in living a full life. Praise and honest appreciation do more than al-most anything else to make people like us. And the same precepts that make us happy in the world will give us a happy home life, too—the first need of every man and woman. ᷣᷢ

≈§JAPANESE PROVERB

ONE KIND WORD can warm three winter months.

≈§GERTRUDE STEIN

I LIKE FAMILIARITY. In me it does not breed contempt. Only more familiarity.

≈§HELEN KELLER

ANYONE WHO, OUT of goodness of his heart, speaks a helpful word, gives a cheering smile, or smooths over a rough place in another's path knows that the delight he feels is so intimate a part of himself that he lives by it. The joy of surmounting obstacles which once seemed unremovable, and pushing the frontier of accomplishment further—what joy is there like unto it? If those who seek happiness would only stop one little minute and think, they would see that the delights they really experience are as countless as the grasses at their feet or the dewdrops sparkling upon the morning flowers.

———————◄(◇(◇(◇(◇)◇)◇)◇)◇———————

from the writings of DALE CARNEGIE

I F WE WANT to find happiness, let's stop thinking about
gratitude or ingratitude and give for the inner joy of
giving.

❧ SENATOR PAUL DOUGLAS

WHEN YOU DIFFER with a man, show him, by your looks, by your
bearing and by everything that you do or say, that you love him.

❧ WILBUR WRIGHT

A PARROT TALKS much but flies little.

❧ EMILY DICKINSON

If I can stop one heart from breaking,
I shall not live in vain;
If I can ease one life the aching,
Or cool one pain,
Or help one fainting robin
Unto his nest again,
I shall not live in vain.

❧ RALPH WALDO EMERSON

THERE IS ALWAYS a best way of doing everything, if it be to boil
an egg. Manners are the happy ways of doing things.

BENJAMIN FRANKLIN

I MADE IT a rule, to forbear all direct contradiction to the sentiments of others, and all positive assertion of my own. I even forbade myself the use of every word or expression in the language that imported a fix'd opinion, such as "certainly," "undoubtedly," etc., and I adopted, instead of them, "I conceive," "I apprehend," or "I imagine" a thing to be so or so; or "it so appears to me at present." When another asserted something that I thought an error, I deny'd myself the pleasure of contradicting him abruptly, and of showing immediately some absurdity in his proposition; and in answering I began by observing that in certain cases or circumstances his opinion would be right, but in the present case there appear'd or seem'd to me some difference, etc. I soon found the advantage of this change in my manner; the conversations I engag'd in went on more pleasantly. The modest way in which I propos'd my opinions procur'd them a readier reception and less contradiction; I had less mortification when I was found to be in the wrong, and I more easily prevail'd with others to give up their mistakes and join with me when I happened to be in the right.

And this mode, which I at first put on with some violence to natural inclination, became at length so easy, and so habitual to me, that perhaps for these fifty years past no one has ever heard a dogmatical expression escape me. And to this habit (after my character of integrity) I think it principally owing that I had early so much weight with my fellow citizens when I proposed new institutions, or alterations in the old, and so much influence in public councils when I became a member; for I was but a bad speaker, never eloquent, subject to much hesitation in my choice of words, hardly correct in language, and yet I generally carried my points.

ᵛᵍTHEODORE ROOSEVELT, JR.

I HAVE ALWAYS had a great respect for a Philippine proverb: "Into the closed mouth the fly does not get."

ᵛᵍLORD CHESTERFIELD

LOOK IN THE face of the person to whom you are speaking if you wish to know his real sentiments, for he can command his words more easily than his countenance.

ᵛᵍRUSSELL LYNES

THE ART OF acceptance is the art of making someone who has done you a small favor wish that he might have done you a greater one.

———————————◊((◊((◊((◻)◊))◊))◊———————————

from the writings of DALE CARNEGIE

THREE-FOURTHS OF the people you will meet tomorrow are hungering and thirsting for sympathy. Give it to them, and they will love you.

ᵛᵍANONYMOUS

KINDNESS IS A language the deaf can hear and the dumb can understand.

ᵛᵍSENECA

WHEREVER THERE IS a human being there is a chance for a kindness.

from the writings of DALE CARNEGIE

REMEMBER THAT THE other man may be totally wrong. But he doesn't think so. Don't condemn him. Any fool can do that. Try to understand him. Only wise, tolerant, exceptional men even try to do that.

There is a reason why the other man thinks and acts as he does. Ferret out that hidden reason—and you have the key to his actions, perhaps to his personality.

Try honestly to put yourself in his place.

GEORGE WASHINGTON

STRIVE NOT WITH your superiors in argument, but always submit your judgment to others with modesty.

BENJAMIN FRANKLIN

A CHEERFUL FACE is nearly as good for an invalid as healthy weather.

BENJAMIN DISRAELI

ONE OF THE hardest things in this world to do is to admit you are wrong. And nothing is more helpful in resolving a situation than its frank admission.

RUSSELL SAGE

THE BEST WAY for a young man who is without friends or influence to begin is: first, to get a position; second, to keep his mouth shut; third, observe; fourth, be faithful; fifth, make his employer think he would be lost in a fog without him; sixth, be polite.

━━━━━━━━◇❨◇❨◇❨◎❩◇❩◇❩◇━━━━━━━━

from the writings of DALE CARNEGIE

IF YOU DO not like people generally, there is one simple
way of cultivating the characteristic: just look for
good traits. You'll be sure to find some.

⋙BENJAMIN FRANKLIN

ANY FOOL CAN criticize, condemn and complain—and most fools do.

⋙FRANÇOIS DE LA ROCHEFOUCAULD

ONE OF THE reasons that we find so few persons rational and
agreeable in conversation is that there is hardly a person who does
not think more of what he wants to say than of his answer to what
is said.

⋙LAO-TSE

THE WISE MAN does not lay up treasure. The more he gives to
others, the more he has for his own.

⋙WILLIAM JAMES

WE ARE NOT only gregarious animals, liking to be in sight of our
fellows, but we have an innate propensity to get ourselves noticed,
and noticed favorably, by our kind. No more fiendish punishment
could be devised, were such a thing physically possible, than that
one should be turned loose in society and remain absolutely un-
noticed by all the members thereof.

✎FRANK SWINNERTON

THE WISEST MAN I have ever known once said to me, "Nine out of every ten people improve on acquaintance"; and I have found his words true.

✎MARCUS AURELIUS

KINDNESS IS IRRESISTIBLE, be it but sincere and no mock smile or mask assumed. For what can the most unconscionable of men do to thee if thou persist in being kindly to him?

✎AESOP

A DISPUTE once arose between the wind and the sun over which was the stronger of the two. There seemed to be no way of settling the issue. But suddenly they saw a traveler coming down the road.

"This is our chance," said the sun, "to prove who is right. Whichever of us can make that man take off his coat shall be the stronger. And just to show you how sure I am, I'll let you have the first chance."

So the sun hid behind a cloud, and the wind blew an icy blast. But the harder he blew the more closely did the traveler wrap his coat around him. At last the wind had to give up in disgust. Then the sun came out from behind the cloud and began to shine down upon the traveler with all his power. The traveler felt the sun's genial warmth, and as he grew warmer and warmer he began to loosen his coat. Finally he was forced to take it off altogether and to sit down in the shade of a tree and fan himself. So the sun was right, after all!

from the writings of DALE CARNEGIE

YOU CAN MAKE more friends in two months by becoming really interested in other people, than you can in two years by trying to get other people interested in you. Which is just another way of saying that the way to make a friend is to be one.

BENJAMIN FRANKLIN

ARGUING IS A game that two can play at. But it is a strange game in that neither opponent ever wins.

LORD CHESTERFIELD

NEVER HOLD ANY one by the button or the hand in order to be heard out; for if people are unwilling to hear you, you had better hold your tongue than them.

ISAAC WATTS

Be you to others kind and true,
As you'd have others be to you,
And neither do nor say to men
Whate'er you would not take again.

ARTHUR SCHOPENHAUER

POLITENESS IS TO human nature what warmth is to wax.

SIR ISAAC NEWTON

WHEN YOU COME into any fresh company, observe their humours. Suit your own carriage thereto, by which insinuation you will make their converse more free and open. Let your discours be more in querys and doubtings than peremptory assertions or disputings, it being the designe of travelers to learne, not to teach. Besides, it will persuade your acquaintance that you have the greater esteem of them, and soe make them more ready to communicate what they know to you; whereas nothing sooner occasions disrespect and quarrels than peremptorinesse. You will find little or no advantage in seeming wiser, or much more ignorant than your company. Seldom discommend anything though never so bad, or doe it but moderately, lest you be unexpectedly forced to an unhansom retraction. It is safer to commend anything more than is due, than to discommend a thing soe much as it deserves; for commendations meet not so often with oppositions, or, at least, are not usually soe ill resented by men that think otherwise, as discommendations; and you will insinuate into men's favour by nothing sooner than seeming to approve and commend what they like; but beware of doing it by a comparison.

SAMUEL GOMPERS

ONE FACT STANDS out in bold relief in the history of men's attempts for betterment. That is that when compulsion is used, only resentment is aroused, and the end is not gained. Only through moral suasion and appeal to men's reason can a movement succeed.

CAMILLO DI CAVOUR

THE MAN WHO trusts men will make fewer mistakes than he who distrusts them.

from the writings of DALE CARNEGIE

HERE ARE SOME suggestions on the art of smiling! First, you must have the right mental attitude toward the world and its people. Until you do, you will not be highly successful. But merely smiling perfunctorily will help, for it will create happiness in others and that will act as a boomerang for you. To generate a pleasant feeling in another will make you feel more pleasant, and pretty soon you will mean that smile.

Also, when you smile, you will be stilling any unpleasant or artificial feeling you may have been experiencing within you. When you smile at another, you are telling him in a subtle way that you like him, at least to some degree. He will get that meaning and he will like you better. Try out the smiling habit. You have nothing to lose.

BENJAMIN FRANKLIN

YEARS HAVE TAUGHT me at least one thing and that is not to try to avoid an unpleasant fact, but rather to grasp it firmly and let the other person observe I am at least treating him fairly. Then he, it has been my observation, will treat me in the same spirit.

CICERO

NOTHING IS MORE becoming in a great man than courtesy and forbearance.

from the writings of DALE CARNEGIE

ONE OF THE surest ways of making a friend and influencing the opinion of another is to give consideration to his opinion, to let him sustain his feeling of importance.

JOHN WANAMAKER

SOME PEOPLE, WITHOUT knowing it, carry with them a magnifying glass, with which they see, when they wish, other people's imperfections.

ALFRED ADLER

A SIMPLE RULE in dealing with those who are hard to get along with is to remember that this person is striving to assert his superiority; and you must deal with him from that point of view.

HENRY BURTON

Have you had a kindness shown?
   Pass it on;
'Twas not given for thee alone,
   Pass it on;
Let it travel down the years,
Let it wipe another's tears,
'Til in Heaven the deed appears—
Pass it on.

⬥⟨⟨⬥⟨⟨⬥⟨⟨⟩⟩⬥⟩⬥⟩⬥

from the writings of DALE CARNEGIE

IF YOU WANT to win friends, make it a point to remember them. If you remember my name, you pay me a subtle compliment; you indicate that I have made an impression on you. Remember my name and you add to my feeling of importance.

⌐§WILLIAM MORRIS

I'M GOING YOUR way, so let us go hand in hand. You help me and I'll help you. We shall not be here very long, for soon death, the kind old nurse, will come back and rock us all to sleep. Let us help one another while we may.

⌐§ALFRED ADLER

YOU CAN BE cured in 14 days [to patients afflicted with melancholia] if you follow this prescription. Try to think every day how you can please someone.

It is the individual who is not interested in his fellow man who has the greatest difficulties in life and provides the greatest injury to others. It is from among such individuals that all human failures spring. All that we demand of a human being, and the highest praise we can give him, is that he should be a good fellow worker, a friend to all other men, and a true partner in love and marriage.

⌐§RALPH WALDO EMERSON

IT IS ONE of the most beautiful compensations of this life that no man can sincerely try to help another without helping himself.

✑ HENRY JAMES

THE FIRST THING to learn in intercourse with others is noninterference with their own peculiar ways of being happy, provided those ways do not assume to interfere by violence with ours.

✑ WOODROW WILSON

IF YOU COME at me with your fists doubled, I think I can promise you that mine will double as fast as yours; but if you come to me and say, "Let us sit down and take counsel together, and, if we differ from one another, understand why it is we differ from one another, just what the points at issue are," we will presently find that we are not so far apart after all, that the points on which we differ are few and the points on which we agree are many, and that if we only have the patience and the candor and the desire to get together, we will get together.

✑ KENNETH M. GOODE

STOP A MINUTE to contrast your keen interest in your own affairs with your mild concern about anything else. Realize then, that everybody else in the world feels exactly the same way! Then, along with Lincoln and Roosevelt, you will have grasped the only solid foundation for any job other than warden in a penitentiary; namely, that success in dealing with people depends on a sympathetic grasp of the other man's viewpoint.

✑ WILLIAM WORDSWORTH

That best portion of a good man's life,
His little, nameless, unremembered acts
Of kindness.

from the writings of DALE CARNEGIE

IF YOU HAVEN'T thought much about courtesy, stop now and give it a thought. Here are some suggestions that will help you to develop an habitually courteous attitude:

(1. When talking with another, listen attentively. Don't assume a bored attitude, or allow an "I knew it" expression to flicker across your features.

(2. Don't interrupt another when talking. Let him talk himself out, even though he be a complainer. If you interrupt him, you are implying that what he is saying isn't worth listening to.

(3. Get the name of the speaker, if he is a stranger to you, and use it when occasion arises.

(4. If the speaker is wrong in a statement, never contradict him flatly. If necessary, mention, after he has finished, that you had always thought thus-and-so, and add that if you have been wrong you are glad to be advised.

(5. Don't assume an air of importance. Never allow the speaker, or your companion, to feel that he is inferior to you in any sense. He won't think himself inferior, and he will resent you if you show that you think he is. If you have had superior advantages, he will attribute that to your luck, not to you.

(6. Apologize when you have been wrong.

from the writings of DALE CARNEGIE

THIS IS A hurried age we're living in. If you've got anything to say, say it quickly, get to the point and stop, and give the other man a chance to talk.

◄§BENJAMIN DISRAELI

TALK TO A man about himself and he will listen for hours.

◄§FRANK IRVING FLETCHER

THE VALUE OF A SMILE AT CHRISTMAS

It costs nothing, but creates much.

It enriches those who receive, without impoverishing those who give.

It happens in a flash and the memory of it sometimes lasts forever.

None are so rich they can get along without it, and none so poor but are richer for its benefits.

It creates happiness in the home, fosters good will in a business, and is the countersign of friends.

It is rest to the weary, daylight to the discouraged, sunshine to the sad, and Nature's best antidote for trouble.

Yet it cannot be bought, begged, borrowed, or stolen, for it is something that is no earthly good to anybody till it is given away!

And if in the last-minute rush of Christmas buying, some of our salespeople should be too tired to give you a smile, may we ask you to leave one of yours?

For nobody needs a smile so much as those who have none left to give!

◈LORD CHESTERFIELD

BE WISER THAN other people, if you can; but do not tell them so.

◈JESUS

DO UNTO OTHERS as you would have others do unto you.

◈WILLIAM LYON PHELPS

WHEN I WAS eight years old and was spending a weekend visiting my Aunt Libby Linsley at her home in Stratford on the Housatonic, a middle-aged man called one evening, and after a polite skirmish with my aunt, he devoted his attention to me. At that time, I happened to be excited about boats, and the visitor discussed the subject in a way that seemed to me particularly interesting. After he left, I spoke of him with enthusiasm. What a man! And how tremendously interested in boats! My aunt informed me he was a New York lawyer; that he cared nothing whatever about boats—took not the slightest interest in the subject. "But why then did he talk all the time about boats?"

"Because he is a gentleman. He saw you were interested in boats, and he talked about the things he knew would interest and please you. He made himself agreeable."

I never forgot my aunt's remark.

◈WALT WHITMAN

HAVE YOU LEARNED lessons only of those who admired you, and were tender with you, and stood aside for you? Have you not learned great lessons from those who rejected you, and braced themselves against you, or disputed the passage with you?

from the writings of DALE CARNEGIE

M AKE A MAN laugh a good hearty laugh, and you've paved the way for friendship. When a man laughs with you, he, to some extent, likes you.

≪ PHILLIPS BROOKS

Y OU WHO ARE letting miserable misunderstandings run on from year to year, meaning to clear them up some day;

You who are keeping wretched quarrels alive because you cannot quite make up your mind that now is the day to sacrifice your pride and kill them;

You who are passing men sullenly upon the street, not speaking to them out of some silly spite, and yet knowing that it would fill you with shame and remorse if you heard that one of those men were dead tomorrow morning;

You who are letting your neighbor starve, till you hear that he is dying of starvation;

Or letting your friend's heart ache for a word of appreciation or sympathy, which you mean to give him some day;

If you only could know and see and feel, all of a sudden, that "the time is short," how it would break the spell! How you would go instantly and do the thing which you might never have another chance to do.

≪ ALBERT SCHWEITZER

ONE THING I know: the only ones among you who will be really happy are those who will have sought and found how to serve.

from the writings of DALE CARNEGIE

D<small>O SOME KINDLY</small> thing for someone every chance you get. At the end of the day add up what it has meant to you. You won't be able to realize all that one kindly deed can mean, but if it does nothing else, it shows someone that you like him and it will certainly make him like you to some degree.

᭵BENJAMIN FRANKLIN

I<small>F YOU ARGUE</small> and rankle and contradict, you may achieve a temporary victory—sometimes; but it will be an empty victory because you will never get your opponent's good will.

᭵JOHN WANAMAKER

T<small>O MISS AN</small> opportunity to do a kind thing, to give someone innocent pleasure or lend a helping hand where needed, if in your power to do so, may be to risk the loss of a happy memory that might sweeten and lighten your way later on.

᭵ABRAHAM LINCOLN

N<small>O MAN WHO</small> is resolved to make the most of himself can spare time for personal contention. Still less can he afford to take the consequences, including the vitiation of his temper and the loss of self-control. Yield larger things to which you show no more than equal rights; and yield lesser ones though clearly your own. Better give your path to a dog than be bitten by him in contesting for the right. Even killing the dog would not cure the bite.

⨳I CORINTHIANS 13

THOUGH I SPEAK with the tongues of men and of angels, and I have not love, I am become as sounding brass, or a tinkling cymbal.

And though I have the gift of prophecy, and understand all mysteries, and all knowledge; and though I have all faith, so that I could remove mountains, and have not love, I am nothing.

And though I bestow all my goods to feed the poor, and though I give my body to be burned, and have not love, it profiteth me nothing.

Love suffereth long, and is kind; love envieth not;

Love vaunteth not itself, is not puffed up, doth not behave itself unseemly, seeketh not her own, is not easily provoked, thinketh no evil;

Rejoiceth not in iniquity, but rejoiceth in the truth;

Beareth all things, believeth all things, hopeth all things, endureth all things.

Love never faileth: but whether there be prophecies, they shall fail; whether there be tongues, they shall cease; whether there be knowledge, it shall vanish away. For we know in part, and we prophesy in part. But when that which is perfect is come, then that which is in part shall be done away.

When I was a child, I spake as a child, I understood as a child, I thought as a child; but when I became a man, I put away childish things.

For now we see through a glass, darkly; but then face to face: now I know in part; but then shall I know even as also I am known.

And now abideth faith, hope, love, these three; but the greatest of these is love.

―――――――――◄‹‹‹‹‹‹‹◊♦♦♦♦◊―――――――――

from the writings of DALE CARNEGIE

IF YOU MAKE an appointment with another, you are really assuming a trust; if you do not keep faith with him, you are stealing from him—not greenbacks out of his wallet, but filching time out of his bank—something that will be lost to him forever.

―――――――――――――――――――――――――――――――

⊷JOHN BOYLE O'REILLY

"What is the real good?"
I ask in musing mood.

"Order," said the law court;
"Knowledge," said the school;
"Truth," said the wise man;
"Pleasure," said the fool;
"Love," said the maiden;
"Beauty," said the page;
"Freedom," said the dreamer;
"Home," said the sage;
"Fame," said the soldier;
"Equity," said the seer.
Spake my heart fully sad:
"The answer is not here."

Then within my bosom
Softly this I heard:
"Each heart holds the secret:
'Kindness' is the word."

⇜WARDEN LEWIS E. LAWES

IF YOU MUST deal with a crook, there is only one possible way of getting the better of him—treat him as if he were an honorable gentleman. Take it for granted he is on the level. He will be so flattered by such treatment that he may answer to it, and be proud that someone trusts him.

⇜FRANÇOIS DE LA ROCHEFOUCAULD

IF YOU WANT enemies, excel your friends; but if you want friends, let your friends excel you.

⇜LAO-TSE

THE REASON WHY rivers and seas receive the homage of a hundred mountain streams is that they keep below them. Thus they are able to reign over all the mountain streams. So the sage, wishing to be above men, putteth himself behind them. Thus, though his place be above men, they do not feel his weight; though his place be before them, they do not count it an injury.

⇜WINSTON CHURCHILL

CONSIDERATION FOR THE lives of others and the laws of humanity, even when one is struggling for one's life and in the greatest stress, does not go wholly unrewarded.

⇜ELBERT HUBBARD

IT IS FOOLISH to say sharp, hasty things, but it is a deal more foolish to write 'em. When a man sends you an impudent letter, sit right down and give it back to him with interest ten times compounded—and then throw both letters in the wastebasket.

from the writings of DALE CARNEGIE

DO YOU KNOW the most important trait a man can have? It is not executive ability; it is not a great mentality; it is not kindliness, nor courage, nor a sense of humor, though each of these is of tremendous importance.

In my opinion, it is the ability to make friends, which, boiled down, means the ability to see the best in man.

MARK TWAIN

IF YOU WISH to lower yourself in a person's favor, one good way is to tell his story over again, the way *you* heard it.

THOMAS À KEMPIS

HOW SELDOM WE weigh our neighbor in the same balance with ourselves.

JULIA CARNEY

> Little drops of water,
> Little grains of sand,
> Make the mighty ocean
> And the pleasant land.
>
> Little deeds of kindness,
> Little words of love,
> Make our world an Eden
> Like the Heaven above.

⋙ABRAHAM LINCOLN

WHEN THE CONDUCT of men is designed to be influenced, persuasion, kind, unassuming persuasion, should ever be adopted. It is an old and a true maxim, that a "drop of honey catches more flies than a gallon of gall." So with men. If you would win a man to your cause, first convince him that you are his sincere friend. Therein is a drop of honey that catches his heart, which, say what he will, is the great high road to his reason, and which, when once gained, you will find but little trouble in convincing his judgment of the justice of your cause, if indeed that cause really be a just one. On the contrary, assume to dictate to his judgment, or to command his action, or to mark him as one to be shunned and despised, and he will retreat within himself, close all the avenues to his head and his heart; and tho' your cause be naked truth itself, transformed to the heaviest lance, harder than steel, and sharper than steel can be made, and tho' you throw it with more than Herculean force and precision, you shall no more be able to pierce him, than to penetrate the hard shell of a tortoise with a rye straw.

Such is man, and so must he be understood by those who would lead him, even to his own best interest. . . .

⋙LORD CHESTERFIELD

THE MANNER OF your speaking is full as important as the matter, as more people have ears to be tickled than understandings to judge.

⋙HENRY WARD BEECHER

"I CAN FORGIVE, but I cannot forget," is only another way of saying, "I will not forgive." A forgiveness ought to be like a canceled note, torn in two and burned up, so that it never can be shown against the man.

✑ANONYMOUS

I SHALL PASS this way but once; any good, therefore, that I can do or any kindness that I can show to any human being, let me do it now. Let me not defer nor neglect it, for I shall not pass this way again.

✑JOHN WANAMAKER

I LEARNED THIRTY years ago that it is foolish to scold. I have enough trouble overcoming my own limitations without fretting over the fact that God has not seen fit to distribute evenly the gift of intelligence.

✑OSCAR WILDE

SELFISHNESS IS NOT living as one wishes to live; it is asking others to live as one wishes to live. And unselfishness is letting other people's lives alone, not interfering with them. Selfishness always aims at creating around it an absolute uniformity of type. Unselfishness recognizes infinite variety of type as a delightful thing, accepts it, acquiesces in it, enjoys it.

---

from the writings of DALE CARNEGIE

DON'T YOU HAVE much more faith in ideas that you discover for yourself than in ideas that are handed to you on a silver platter? If so, isn't it bad judgment to try to ram your opinions down the throats of other people? Wouldn't it be wiser to make suggestions—and let the other man think out the conclusion for himself?

from the writings of DALE CARNEGIE

WE OUGHT TO be modest, for neither you nor I amount to much. Both of us will pass on and be completely forgotten a century from now. Life is too short to bore other people with talk of our petty accomplishments. Let's encourage them to talk instead.

LORD CHESTERFIELD

MANNERS MUST ADORN knowledge, and smooth its way in the world; without them it is like a great rough diamond, very well in a closet by way of curiosity, and also for its intrinsic value; but most prized when polished.

OLIVER WENDELL HOLMES

TALKING IS LIKE playing on the harp; there is as much in laying the hand on the strings to stop their vibrations as in twanging them to bring out their music.

ALFRED E. SMITH

BE SINCERE. BE simple in words, manners and gestures. Amuse as well as instruct. If you can make a man laugh, you can make him think and make him like and believe you.

HORACE MANN

DO NOT THINK of knocking out another person's brains because he differs in opinion from you. It would be as rational to knock yourself on the head because you differ from yourself ten years ago.

—◆(◇◆(◇◆(◇)◆>)◆>)◆—

from the writings of DALE CARNEGIE

Y OU CAN TELL a man he is wrong by a look or an in-
tonation or a gesture just as eloquently as you can in
words—and if you tell him he is wrong, do you make him
want to agree with you? Never! For you have struck a
direct blow at his intelligence, his judgment, his pride, his
self-respect. That will make him want to strike back.
But it will never make him want to change his mind. You
may then hurl at him all the logic of a Plato or an Im-
manuel Kant, but you will not alter his opinion, for you
have hurt his feelings.

⊸§ JOSEPH ADDISON

T HE TRUE ART of being agreeable is to appear well pleased with
all the company, and rather to seem well entertained with them
than to bring entertainment to them. A man thus disposed may
have not much learning, nor any wit; but if he has common sense,
and something friendly in his behavior, it conciliates men's minds
more than the brightest parts without this disposition.

⊸§ SENECA

THE MANNER OF saying or of doing anything goes a great way in
the value of the thing itself. It was well said of him that called
a good office, if done harshly and with an ill will, a stony piece
of bread: "It is necessary for him that is hungry to receive it, but
it almost chokes a man in the going down."

✑CHARLES SCHWAB

IN MY WIDE association in life, meeting with many and great men in various parts of the world, I have yet to find the man, however great or exalted his station, who did not do better work and put forth greater effort under a spirit of approval than he would ever do under a spirit of criticism.

✑CHINESE PROVERB

A BIT OF fragrance always clings to the hand that gives you roses.

✑THOMAS DREIER

ONE THING SCIENTISTS have discovered is that often-praised children become more intelligent than often-blamed ones. If some of your employees are a bit dumb, perhaps your treatment of them is to blame. There's a creative element in praise.

✑WILLIAM JAMES

THE DEEPEST PRINCIPLE in human nature is the craving to be appreciated.

✑CHARLES SCHWAB

I CONSIDER MY ability to arouse enthusiasm among men the greatest asset I possess, and the way to develop the best in a man is by appreciation and encouragement.

There is nothing else that so kills the ambition of a man as criticism from his superiors. I never criticize anyone. I believe in giving a man incentive to work. So I am anxious to praise but loath to find fault. If I like anything, I am hearty in my appreciation and lavish in my praise.

from the writings of DALE CARNEGIE

D<small>O YOU FEEL</small> that you are superior to the Japanese? The truth is that the Japanese consider themselves far superior to you. A conservative Japanese, for example, is infuriated at the sight of a white man dancing with a Japanese lady.

Do you consider yourself superior to the Hindus in India? That is your privilege; but a million Hindus feel so infinitely superior to you that they wouldn't befoul themselves by condescending to touch food that your heathen shadow had fallen across and contaminated.

Do you feel you are superior to the Eskimos? Again, that is your privilege; but would you really like to know what the Eskimo thinks of you? Well, there are a few native hobos among the Eskimos, worthless bums who refuse to work. The Eskimos call them "white men"— that being their utmost term of contempt.

Each nation feels superior to other nations. That breeds patriotism—and wars.

The unvarnished truth is that almost every man you meet feels himself superior to you in some way; and a sure way to his heart is to let him realize in some subtle way that you recognize his importance in his little world, and recognize it sincerely.

SAMUEL JOHNSON

G<small>OD HIMSELF, SIR</small>, does not propose to judge man until the end of his days.

◆MARK TWAIN

KEEP AWAY FROM people who try to belittle your ambitions. Small people always do that, but the really great make you feel that you, too, can become great.

◆GEORGE WASHINGTON

TRUE FRIENDSHIP IS a plant of slow growth, and must undergo and withstand the shocks of adversity before it is entitled to the appellation.

◆RALPH WALDO EMERSON

HAPPINESS IS A perfume which you can't pour on someone without getting some on yourself.

◆HENRY WARD BEECHER

IT IS ONE of the severest tests of friendship to tell your friend of his faults. If you are angry with a man, or hate him, it is not hard to go to him and stab him with words; but so to love a man that you cannot bear to see the stain of sin upon him, and to speak painful truth through loving words—this is friendship. But few have such friends. Our enemies usually teach us what we are, at the point of the sword.

◆WILLIAM SHAKESPEARE

Those friends thou hast, and their adoption tried,
Grapple them to thy soul with hoops of steel;
But do not dull thy palm with entertainment
Of each new-hatched, unfledged comrade.

from the writings of DALE CARNEGIE

REMEMBER THAT THE man you are talking to is a hundred times more interested in himself and his wants and his problems than he is in you and your problems. His toothache means more to him than a famine in China that kills a million people. A boil on his neck interests him more than forty earthquakes in Africa. Think of that the next time you start a conversation.

JEAN DE LA BRUYÈRE

TWO PERSONS CANNOT long be friends if they cannot forgive each other's little failings.

WILLIAM PENN

A TRUE FRIEND unbosoms freely, advises justly, assists readily, adventures boldly, takes all patiently, defends courageously, and continues a friend unchangeably.

HENRY DAVID THOREAU

EVEN THE UTMOST goodwill and harmony and practical kindness are not sufficient for Friendship, for Friends do not live in harmony merely, as some say, but in melody. We do not wish for Friends to feed and clothe our bodies—neighbors are kind enough for that—but to do the like office to our spirits.

SIR PHILIP SIDNEY

THERE IS NOTHING so great that I fear to do it for my friend; nothing so small that I will disdain to do it for him.

⊰WILLIAM PENN

THERE CAN BE no friendship where there is no freedom. Friendship loves a free air, and will not be fenced up in strait and narrow enclosures.

⊰RALPH WALDO EMERSON

A FRIEND IS a person with whom I may be sincere. Before him I may think aloud. I am arrived at last in the presence of a man so real and equal that I may drop even those undermost garments of dissimulation, courtesy, and second thought, which men never put off, and may deal with him with the simplicity and wholeness with which one chemical atom meets another. Sincerity is the luxury allowed, like diadems and authority, only to the highest rank, that being permitted to speak truth, as having none above it to court or conform unto. Every man alone is sincere. At the entrance of a second person, hypocrisy begins. We parry and fend the approach of our fellow man by compliments, by gossip, by amusements, by affairs. We cover up our thought from him under a hundred folds. . . . Almost every man we meet requires some civility, requires to be humored—he has some fame, some talent, some whim of religion or philanthropy in his head that is not to be questioned, and which spoils all conversation with him. But a friend is a sane man who exercises not my ingenuity but me. My friend gives me entertainment without requiring me to stoop, or to lisp, or to mask myself. A friend therefore is a paradox in nature. I who alone am, I who see nothing in nature whose existence I can affirm with equal evidence to my own, behold now the semblance of my being, in all its height, variety and curiosity, reiterated in a foreign form; so that a friend may well be reckoned the masterpiece of nature.

⇜§THOMAS JEFFERSON

THE HAPPIEST MOMENTS my heart knows are those in which it is pouring fourth its affections to a few esteemed characters.

⇜§POPE LEO XIII

NO ONE IS so rich that he does not need another's help; no one so poor as not to be useful in some way to his fellow man; and the disposition to ask assistance from others with confidence and to grant it with kindness, is part of our very nature.

⇜§JOHN DRYDEN

Friendship, of itself a holy tie,
Is made more sacred by adversity.

---

from the writings of DALE CARNEGIE

ACTIONS SPEAK LOUDER than words, and a smile says, "I like you. You make me happy. I am glad to see you."

That is why dogs make such a hit. They are so glad to see us that they almost jump out of their skins. So, naturally, we are glad to see them.

An insincere grin? No. That doesn't fool anybody. We know it is mechanical and we resent it. I am talking about a real smile, a heartwarming smile, a smile that comes from within, the kind of smile that will bring a good price in the market place.

from the writings of DALE CARNEGIE

THERE is only one way under high Heaven to get any-body to do anything. Did you ever stop to think of that? Yes, just one way. And that is by making the other person want to do it.

Remember there is no other way.

Of course, you can make a man want to give you his watch by sticking a revolver in his ribs. You can make an employee give you co-operation—until your back is turned—by threatening to fire him. You can make a child do what you want it to do by a whip or a threat. But these crude methods have sharply undesirable repercussions.

The only way I can get you to do anything is by giving you what you want.

EDWIN MARKHAM

There is a destiny that makes us brothers:
None goes his way alone;
All that we send into the lives of others
Comes back into our own.

EDVARD GRIEG

IT IS GREAT to have friends when one is young, but indeed it is still more so when you are getting old. When we are young, friends are, like everything else, a matter of course. In the old days we know what it means to have them.

from the writings of DALE CARNEGIE

WHY, I WONDER, don't we use the same common sense when trying to change people that we use when trying to change dogs? Why don't we use meat instead of a whip? Why don't we use praise instead of condemnation? Let's praise even the slightest improvement. That inspires the other fellow to keep on improving.

RALPH WALDO EMERSON

WE TAKE CARE of our health, we lay up money, we make our roof tight, and our clothing sufficient, but who provides wisely that he shall not be wanting in the best property of all—friends?

JEREMY TAYLOR

FRIENDSHIP IS THE allay of our sorrows, the ease of our passions, the discharge of our oppressions, the sanctuary to our calamities, the counselor of our doubts, the clarity of our minds, the emission of our thoughts, the exercise and improvement of what we meditate.

EPICURUS

IT IS NOT so much our friends' help that helps us as the confidence of their help.

THOMAS À KEMPIS

A WISE LOVER values not so much the gift of the lover as the love of the giver.

⋅ᵛHENRY WARD BEECHER

DO NOT KEEP the alabaster boxes of your love and tenderness sealed up until your friends are dead. Fill their lives with sweetness. Speak approving, cheering words while their ears can hear them and while their hearts can be thrilled by them.

---

from the writings of DALE CARNEGIE

YOU HAVE IT easily in your power to increase the sum total of this world's happiness now. How? By giving a few words of sincere appreciation to someone who is lonely or discouraged. Perhaps you will forget tomorrow the kind words you say today, but the recipient may cherish them over a lifetime.

⋅ᵛCYRUS

ALL MEN HAVE their frailties; and whoever looks for a friend without imperfections, will never find what he seeks. We love ourselves notwithstanding our faults, and we ought to love our friends in like manner.

⋅ᵛJOSEPH ADDISON

FRIENDSHIP IMPROVES HAPPINESS, and abates misery, by doubling our joy, and dividing our grief.

from the writings of DALE CARNEGIE

LET'S CEASE THINKING of our accomplishments, our wants. Let's try to figure out the other man's good points. Then forget flattery. Give honest, sincere appreciation. Be "hearty in your approbation and lavish in your praise," and people will cherish your words and treasure them and repeat them over a lifetime—repeat them years after you have forgotten them.

THOMAS JEFFERSON

I FIND THAT friendship is like wine. It is raw when new. When riped with age it is the true old man's restorative cordial.

AESOP

A HUSBANDMAN WHO had a quarrelsome family, after having tried in vain to reconcile them by words, thought he might more readily prevail by an example. So he called his sons and bade them lay a bundle of sticks before him. Then having tied them up into a fagot, he told the lads, one after another, to take it up and break it. They all tried, but tried in vain. Then, untying the fagot, he gave them the sticks to break one by one. This they did with the greatest ease. Then said the father: "Thus, my sons, as long as you remain united, you are a match for all your enemies; but differ and separate, and you are undone."

⋙RALPH WALDO EMERSON

Our friendships hurry to short and poor conclusions, because we have made them a texture of wine and dreams, instead of the tough fiber of the human heart. The laws of friendship are great, austere, and eternal, of one web with the laws of nature and of morals. But we have aimed at a swift and petty benefit, to such a sudden sweetness. We snatch at the slowest fruit in the whole garden of God, which many summers and many winters must ripen. We seek our friend not sacredly, but with an adulterate passion which would appropriate him to ourselves.

I do not wish to treat friendships daintily, but with roughest courage. When they are real, they are not glass threads or frostwork, but the solidest thing we know.

The end of friendship is a commerce the most strict and homely that can be joined; more strict than any of which we have experienced. It is for aid and comfort through all the relations and passages of life and death. It is fit for serene days, and graceful gifts, and country rambles, but also for rough roads and hard fare, shipwreck, poverty and persecution. It keeps company with the sallies of the wit and the trances of religion. We are to dignify to each other the daily needs and offices of man's life, and embellish it by courage, wisdom and unity. It should never fall into something usual and settled, but should be alert and inventive, and add rhyme and reason to what was drudgery.

⋙HENRY WADSWORTH LONGFELLOW

I breathed a song into the air
It fell to earth, I know not where. . . .
And the song, from beginning to end,
I found again in the heart of a friend.

─────◆《《◆《◆《◎》◆》◆》◆─────

from the writings of DALE CARNEGIE

PRAISE A MAN for what he does well, then gradually help him with his shortcomings. That method will work in an office, in a factory, in one's home, with wife, children, parents, with almost anyone in the world.

───────────────────────────────

SAMUEL JOHNSON

IF A MAN does not make new acquaintances as he advances through life, he will soon find himself left alone. A man should keep his friendships in constant repair.

To let friendship die away by negligence and silence is certainly not wise. It is voluntarily to throw away one of the greatest comforts of this weary pilgrimage.

ELBERT HUBBARD

YOUR FRIEND IS the man who knows all about you, and still likes you.

ASHLEY MONTAGU

WHEN MEN ABANDON the upbringing of their children to their wives, a loss is suffered by everyone, but most of all by themselves. For what they lose is the possibility of growth in themselves for being human which the stimulation of bringing up one's children gives.

FRANK DEMPSTER SHERMAN

It is my joy in life to find
At every turning of the road
The strong arm of a comrade kind
To help me onward with my load.

And since I have no gold to give,
And love alone must make amends,
My only prayer is, while I live—
God make me worthy of my friends.

BERTRAND RUSSELL

SPEAKING PERSONALLY, I have found the happiness of parenthood greater than any other that I have experienced.

(NOTE: *Lord Russell adds the 1959 postscript, "This is no longer true. I have since found greater happiness in marriage."*)

---

from the writings of DALE CARNEGIE

IF YOU AND I want to stir up a resentment tomorrow that may rankle across the decades and endure until death, just let us indulge in a little stinging criticism—no matter how certain we are that it is justified.

When dealing with people, let us remember we are not dealing with creatures of logic. We are dealing with creatures of emotion, creatures bristling with prejudices and motivated by pride and vanity.

⋙KAHLIL GIBRAN

LET THERE BE spaces in your togetherness.

⋙MRS. WALTER DAMROSCH

NEXT TO CARE in choosing a partner, I should place courtesy after marriage. If young wives would only be as courteous to their husbands as to strangers! Any man will run from a shrewish tongue.

⋙EDDIE CANTOR

I OWE MORE to my wife than to anyone else in the world. She was my best pal as a boy; she helped me to go straight. And after we married she saved every dollar, and invested it, and reinvested it. She built up a fortune for me. We have five lovely children. And she's made a wonderful home for me always. If I've gotten anywhere, give her the credit.

⋙IVAN TURGENEV

I WOULD GIVE up all my genius, and all my books, if there were only some woman, somewhere, who cared whether or not I came home late for dinner.

⋙SAMUEL JOHNSON

TO BE HAPPY at home is the ultimate aim of all ambition; the end to which every enterprise and labor tends, and of which every desire prompts the prosecution.

⋙HENRY VAN DYKE

EVERY HOUSE WHERE love abides and friendship is a guest, is surely home, and home, sweet home; for there the heart can rest.

from the writings of DALE CARNEGIE

WOMEN ATTACH A lot of importance to birthdays and anniversaries—just why will forever remain one of those feminine mysteries. The average man can blunder through life without memorizing many dates, but there are a few which are indispensable: 1492, 1776, the date of his wife's birthday, and the year and date of his own marriage. If need be, he can even get along without the first two—but not the last!

ELIZABETH BARRETT BROWNING

How do I love thee? Let me count the ways.
I love thee to the depth and breadth and height
My soul can reach, when feeling out of sight
For the ends of Being and ideal Grace.
I love thee to the level of every day's
Most quiet need, by sun and candlelight.
I love thee freely, as men strive for Right;
I love thee purely, as men turn from Praise;
I love thee with the passion put to use
In my old griefs, and with my childhood's faith.
I love thee with a love I seemed to lose
With my lost saints,—I love thee with the breath,
Smiles, tears, of all my life!—and, if God choose,
I shall but love thee better after death.

from the writings of DALE CARNEGIE

IF YOU FEEL that your marriage may go on the rocks, why not list the things your partner has that are pleasing to you, and opposite set down those traits of your own that might make you a bit difficult to live with. It may change your entire existence.

ALEXANDER HAMILTON

SIX THINGS ARE requisite to create a "happy home." Integrity must be the architect, and tidiness the upholsterer. It must be warmed by affection, lighted up with cheerfulness; and industry must be the ventilator, renewing the atmosphere and bringing in fresh salubrity day by day; while over all, as a protecting canopy and glory, nothing will suffice except the blessing of God.

THE BOOK OF COMMON PRAYER

TO HAVE AND to hold from this day forward, for better, for worse, for richer, for poorer, in sickness and in health, to love and to cherish, till death us do part.

A. EDWARD NEWTON

IF THIS WORLD affords true happiness, it is to be found in a home where love and confidence increase with the years, where the necessities of life come without severe strain, where luxuries enter only after their cost has been carefully considered.

⊷JANE ADDAMS

AMERICA'S FUTURE WILL be determined by the home and the school. The child becomes largely what it is taught, hence we must watch what we teach it, and how we live before it.

⊷JOHN KEBLE

SWEET IS THE smile of home; the mutual look, when hearts are of each other sure.

⊷JEAN PAUL RICHTER

THE GRANDEST OF heroic deeds are those which are performed within four walls and in domestic privacy.

⊷THOMAS BROWNE

TRUE AFFECTION IS a body of enigmas, mysteries and riddles, wherein two so become one that they both become two.

⊷EXODUS 20:12

HONOR THY FATHER and thy mother: that thy days may be long upon the land which the Lord thy God giveth thee.

⊷THOMAS HOOD

Peace and rest at length have come,
All the day's long toil is past;
And each heart is whispering, "Home,
Home at last!"

from the writings of DALE CARNEGIE

DON'T BEAR GRUDGES. Don't be afraid to give in when there is little or nothing at stake. It's the little man who takes pride in his stubbornness, it's the man with the big nature who is willing to shake hands and say it was his fault and offer to start over.

✑§PLATO

DO NOT TRAIN boys to learning by force and harshness, but lead them by what amuses them, so that they may better discover the bent of their minds.

✑§JEREMY TAYLOR

LET HUSBAND AND wife infinitely avoid a curious distinction of mine and thine, for this hath caused all the laws, and all the suits, and all the wars in the world.

✑§MATTHEW VII

THE RAIN DESCENDED, and the floods came, and the winds blew, and beat upon that house; and it fell not: for it was founded upon a rock.

✑§THOMAS FULLER

The good or ill hap of a good or ill life
Is the good or ill choice of a good or ill wife.

⊸§WILLIAM SHAKESPEARE

Let me not to the marriage of true minds
Admit impediments. Love is not love
Which alters when it alteration finds,
Or bends with the remover to remove.
O, no! it is an ever-fixed mark
That looks on tempests and is never shaken;
It is the star to every wandering bark,
Whose worth's unknown, although his height be taken.
Love's not Time's fool, though rosy lips and cheeks
Within his bending sickle's compass come;
Love alters not with his brief hours and weeks,
But bears it out even to the edge of doom.
    If this be error and upon me proved,
    I never writ, nor no man ever loved.

---

from the writings of DALE CARNEGIE

DON'T LAUGH AT a child's ambitions. There is no sting so sharp as ridicule, and a laugh is often ridicule to a child. What a parent should do when he knows his child is overreaching, is to talk it over with him from every angle, and, if possible, find an angle from which the job can be attacked with hope of success. Then urge him forward, give him every encouragement.

Above all, don't help your child to do something that he can accomplish on his own. Don't deny him the priceless privilege and thrill of developing his own success.

from the writings of DALE CARNEGIE

IF YOU CAN be kind and considerate for one day, then you can be for another. It won't cost you a penny in the world. Begin today.

LUTHER BURBANK

IF WE HAD paid no more attention to our plants than we have to our children, we would now be living in a jungle of weeds.

EPHESIANS 5:25

HUSBANDS, LOVE YOUR wives, even as Christ also loved the Church, and gave himself for it.

JEREMY TAYLOR

A HUSBAND'S POWER over his wife is paternal and friendly, not magisterial and despotic.

SIR WALTER SCOTT

AFFECTION CAN WITHSTAND very severe storms of vigor, but not a long polar frost of indifference.

ANTOINE DE SAINT-EXUPÉRY

LOVE DOES NOT consist in gazing at each other but in looking outward together in the same direction.

JOHN DAVIES

Every true wife hath an indented heart,
Wherein the covenants of love are writ,
Whereof her husband keeps the counterpart,
And reads his comforts and his joys in it.

JEAN PAUL RICHTER

WHAT A FATHER says to his children is not heard by the world, but it will be heard by posterity.

HENRY WARD BEECHER

IF GOD HAS taught us all truth in teaching us to love, then he has given us an interpretation of our whole duty to our households. We are not born as the partridge in the wood, or the ostrich of the desert, to be scattered everywhere; but we are to be grouped together, and brooded by love, and reared day by day in that first of churches, the family.

THÉOPHILE GAUTIER

TO RENOUNCE YOUR individuality, to see with another's eyes, to hear with another's ears, to be two and yet but one, to so melt and mingle that you no longer know you are you or another, to constantly absorb and constantly radiate, to reduce earth, sea and sky and all that in them is to a single being so wholly that nothing whatever is withheld, to be prepared at any moment for sacrifice, to double your personality in bestowing it—that is love.

SYDNEY SMITH

A COMFORTABLE HOUSE is a great source of happiness. It ranks immediately after health and a good conscience.

ROBERT LOUIS STEVENSON

A HINT TAKEN, a look understood, conveys the gist of long and delicate explanations; and where the life is known, even yea and nay become luminous. In the closest of all relations—that of a love well-founded and equally shared—speech is half discarded, like a roundabout infantile process or a ceremony of formal etiquette; and the two communicate directly by their presences, and with few looks and fewer words contrive to share their good and evil and uphold each other's hearts in joy. For love rests upon a physical basis; it is a familiarity of nature's making and apart from voluntary choice. Understanding has in some sort outrun knowledge, for the affection perhaps began with the acquaintance; and as it was not made like other relations, so it is not, like them, to be perturbed or clouded. Each knows more than can be uttered; each lives by faith, and believes by a natural compulsion; and between man and wife the language of the body is largely developed and grown strangely eloquent. The thought that prompted and was conveyed in a caress would only lose to be set down in words—ay, although Shakespeare himself should be the scribe.

BRAHMA

WHEN THE ONE man loves the one woman and the one woman loves the one man, the very angels leave heaven and come and sit in that house and sing for joy.

SAMUEL JOHNSON

NO MONEY IS better spent than what is laid out for domestic satisfaction. A man is pleased that his wife is dressed as well as other people, and the wife is pleased that she is so dressed.

from the writings of DALE CARNEGIE

FORGET YOURSELF BY becoming interested in others.
Do every day a good deed that will put a smile of joy
on someone's face.

⋲§ GEORGE BERNARD SHAW

THIS IS TRUE joy of life—the being used for a purpose that is recognized by yourself as a mighty one, instead of being a feverish,
selfish little clod of ailments and grievances, complaining that the
world will not devote itself to making you happy.

⋲§ BENJAMIN FRANKLIN

A SINGLE MAN has not nearly the value he would have in a state
of union. He is an incomplete animal. He resembles the odd half
of a pair of scissors.

⋲§ ABRAHAM LINCOLN

WHATEVER WOMAN MAY cast her lot with mine, should any ever do
so, it is my intention to do all in my power to make her happy and
contented; and there is nothing I can imagine that would make
me more unhappy than to fail in the effort.

⋲§ JOHN SHEFFIELD

The truest joys they seldome prove,
    Who free from quarrels live;
'Tis the most tender part of love,
    Each other to forgive.

from the writings of DALE CARNEGIE

THERE IS ONLY one way under high heaven to get the best of an argument—and that is to avoid it. Avoid it as you would avoid rattlesnakes and earthquakes.

Nine times out of ten, an argument ends with each of the contestants being more firmly convinced than ever that he is absolutely right.

You can't win an argument. You can't because if you lose it, you lose it; and if you win it, you lose it. Why? Well, suppose you triumph over the other man and shoot his argument full of holes and prove that he is *non compos mentis*. Then what? You will feel fine. But what about him? You have made him feel inferior. You have hurt his pride. He will resent your triumph.

THOMAS SPRAT

A GREAT PROPORTION of the wretchedness which has embittered married life has originated in a negligence of trifles. Connubial happiness is a thing of too fine a texture to be handled roughly. It is a sensitive plant, which will not bear even the touch of unkindness; a delicate flower, which indifference will chill and suspicion blast. It must be watered by the showers of tender affection, expanded by the cheering glow of kindness, and guarded by the impregnable barrier of unshaken confidence. Thus matured, it will bloom with fragrance in every season of life, and sweeten even the loneliness of declining years.

ᴥᣚ *THE TATLER*

WHEN TWO PERSONS have so good an opinion of each other as to come together for life, they will not differ in matters of importance, because they think of each other with respect; and in regard to all things of consideration that may affect them, they are prepared for mutual assistance and relief in such occurrences. For less occasions, they form no resolutions, but leave their minds unprepared.

ᣚCALVIN COOLIDGE

FROM OUR BEING together we seemed naturally to come to care for each other. We became engaged in the early summer of 1905 and were married at her home in Burlington, Vermont, on October fourth of that year. I have seen so much fiction written on this subject that I may be pardoned for relating the plain facts. We thought we were made for each other. For almost a quarter of a century she has borne with my infirmities, and I have rejoiced in her graces.

ᣚ THOMAS CARLYLE

IN HER BRIGHT existence she had more sorrows than are common, but also a soft amiability, a capacity for discernment and a noble loyalty of heart, which are rare. For forty years she was the true and loving helpmate of her husband, and by act and word unweariedly forwarded him as none else could have done in all of worth that he did or attempted.

⌇DR. WILLIAM C. MENNINGER

ALL OF OUR findings in psychiatric experience verify the general principles so widely known and so often forgotten, namely—the most desirable satisfactions in life cannot be bought with money. . . . Constantly we must remind ourselves that in the final analysis, one simply cannot purchase sincerity, devotion, dedication or loyalty.

The most important job satisfaction depends on each one having the chance to develop the kind of relationship with his associates that will result in mutual respect and confidence.

4

Work, hard absorbing work, joyous rewarding work—how long have men realized its place in life! And when challenged by a job that seems too big—perseverance is half the battle. ॐ

VOLTAIRE

WORK KEEPS AT bay three great evils: boredom, vice and need.

THOMAS A. EDISON

I NEVER DID a day's work in my life. It was all fun.

GIAN-CARLO MENOTTI

HELL BEGINS ON the day when God grants us a clear vision of all that we might have achieved, of all the gifts which we have wasted, of all that we might have done which we did not do. . . .

For me the conception of Hell lies in two words: *Too late.*

DWIGHT D. EISENHOWER

LIFE IS CERTAINLY only worth while as it represents struggle for worthy causes. There is no struggle in perfect security. I am quite certain that the human being could not continue to exist if he had perfect security.

—————————◦⟨◦⟨◦⟨☐⟩◦⟩◦⟩◦—————————

from the writings of DALE CARNEGIE

BY THINKING THE right thoughts, you can make any job less distasteful. Your boss wants you to be interested in your job so that he will make more money. But let's forget about what the boss wants. Think only of what getting interested in your job will do for you. Remind yourself that it may double the amount of happiness you get out of life, for you spend about one half of your waking hours at your work, and if you don't find happiness in your work, you may never find it anywhere. Keep reminding yourself that getting interested in your job will take your mind off your worries, and, in the long run, will probably bring promotion and increased pay. Even if it doesn't do that, it will reduce fatigue to a minimum and help you enjoy your hours of leisure.

———————————————————————

HELEN KELLER

LOOK WHERE WE will, we find the hand in time and history, working, building, inventing, bringing civilization out of barbarism. The hand symbolizes power and the excellence of work. The mechanic's hand, that minister of elemental forces, the hand that hews, saws, cuts, builds, is useful in the world equally with the delicate hand that paints a wild flower or molds a Grecian urn, or the hand of a statesman that writes a law. The eye cannot say to the hand, "I have no need of thee." Blessed be the hand! Thrice blessed be the hands that work!

↜HENRY WARD BEECHER

WHEN GOD WANTED sponges and oysters, He made them, and put one on a rock, and the other in the mud. When He made man, He did not make him to be a sponge or an oyster; He made him with feet and hands, and head and heart, and vital blood, and a place to use them and said to him, "Go work!"

↜RALPH BARTON PERRY

THERE IS NO BOREDOM like that which can afflict people who are free, and nothing else.

↜CALVIN COOLIDGE

ALL GROWTH DEPENDS upon activity. There is no development physically or intellectually without effort, and effort means work. Work is not a curse; it is the prerogative of intelligence, the only means to manhood and the measure of civilization.

↜KAHLIL GIBRAN

IF YOU CANNOT work with love but only with distaste, it is better that you should leave your work and sit at the gate of the temple and take alms of those who work with joy.

---

from the writings of DALE CARNEGIE

DO THE HARD jobs first. The easy jobs will take care of themselves.

~§CHARLES EVANS HUGHES

I KNOW HARDLY anyone who works too hard. I believe in hard work and long hours of work. Men do not break down from overwork, but from worry and from plunging into dissipation and efforts not aligned with their work.

---

from the writings of DALE CARNEGIE

IF YOU ACT "as if" you are interested in your job, that bit of acting will tend to make your interest real. It will also tend to decrease your fatigue, your tensions, and your worries.

~§JOHN D. ROCKEFELLER

THE MAN WHO starts out simply with the idea of getting rich won't succeed; you must have a larger ambition. There is no mystery in business success. . . . If you do each day's task successfully, and stay faithfully within these natural operations of commercial laws which I talk so much about, and keep your head clear, you will come out all right.

~§HENRY WADSWORTH LONGFELLOW
Each morning sees some task begun,
Each evening sees it close;
Something attempted, something done,
Has earned a night's repose.

—◄‹◦‹◦‹◦›◦›◦›►—

from the writings of DALE CARNEGIE

GET BUSY. KEEP busy. It's the cheapest kind of medicine there is on this earth—and one of the best.

ALEXANDER GRAHAM BELL

KNOW WHAT WORK you want to do and go after it. The young man who gets ahead must decide for himself what he wishes to do. From his own tastes, his own enthusiasm, he must get the motive and the inspiration which are to start him on his way to a successful life.

WILLIAM LYON PHELPS

ONE OF THE chief reasons for success in life is the ability to maintain a daily interest in one's work, to have a chronic enthusiasm, to regard each day as important.

THEODORE ROOSEVELT

I DON'T PITY any man who does hard work worth doing. I admire him. I pity the creature who doesn't work, at whichever end of the social scale he may regard himself as being.

RALPH WALDO EMERSON

WHEN I GO into my garden with a spade, and dig a bed, I feel such an exhilaration and health that I discover that I have been defrauding myself all this time in letting others do for me what I should have done with my own hands.

◄§JOHN RUSKIN

WHEN MEN ARE rightly occupied, their amusement grows out of their work, as the color petals out of a fruitful flower; when they are faithfully helpful and compassionate, all their emotions are steady, deep, perpetual and vivifying to the soul as is the natural pulse to the body.

◄§SIR THEODORE MARTIN

WORK IS THE true elixir of life. The busiest man is the happiest man. Excellence in any art or profession is attained only by hard and persistent work. Never believe that you are perfect. When a man imagines, even after years of striving, that he has attained perfection, his decline begins.

◄§RALPH WALDO EMERSON

SUCCESS IN YOUR work, the finding a better method, the better understanding that insures the better performing is hat and coat, is food and wine, is fire and horse and health and holiday. At least, I find that any success in my work has the effect on my spirits of all these.

---

from the writings of DALE CARNEGIE

ARE YOU BORED with life? Then throw yourself into some work you believe in with all your heart, live for it, die for it, and you'll find a happiness that you had thought could never be yours.

from the writings of DALE CARNEGIE

DON'T BE AFRAID to give your best to what seemingly are small jobs. Every time you conquer one it makes you that much stronger. If you do the little jobs well, the big ones will tend to take care of themselves.

DAVID GRAYSON

HAPPINESS, I HAVE discovered, is nearly always a rebound from hard work. It is one of the follies of men to imagine that they can enjoy mere thought, or emotion, or sentiment. As well try to eat beauty! For happiness must be tricked! She loves to see men at work. She loves sweat, weariness, self-sacrifice. . . .

There is something fine in hard physical labor. . . . One actually stops thinking. I often work long without any thought whatever, so far as I know, save that connected with the monotonous repetition of the labor itself—down with the spade, out with it, up with it, over with it—and repeat.

And yet sometimes—mostly in the forenoon when I am not at all tired—I will suddenly have a sense as of the world opening around me—a sense of its beauty and its meanings—giving me a peculiar deep happiness, that is near complete content.

WILLIAM JAMES

THE MAN WHOSE acquisitions stick is the man who is always achieving and advancing whilst his neighbors, spending most of their time in relearning what they once knew but have forgotten, simply hold their own.

⋙ WILLIAM JAMES

LET NO YOUTH have any anxiety about the upshot of his education, whatever the line of it may be. If he keeps faithfully busy
each hour of the working day, he may safely leave the final result
to itself. He can, with perfect certainty, count on waking up some
fine morning to find himself one of the competent ones of his
generation, in whatever pursuit he may have singled out.

---

from the writings of DALE CARNEGIE

A SHOCKINGLY LARGE number of our worries and our
hidden tensions stem from the fact that millions
of people have never found themselves, have never discovered the kind of work they could love and do well. Instead, they seethe with inner rebellion because they spend
their lives doing work they despise.

⋙ RALPH WALDO EMERSON

WORK AND THOU canst not escape the reward; whether thy work
be fine or coarse, planting corn or writing epics, so only it be honest
work, done to thine own approbation, it shall earn a reward to
the senses as well as to the thought. No matter how often defeated,
you are born to victory. The reward of a thing well done is to
have done it.

from the writings of DALE CARNEGIE

ARE YOU DOING the work you like best? If not, do something about it! You will never achieve real success unless you like what you are doing. Many men who have achieved success have had to try several things before they knew what they wanted to do.

THOMAS A. EDISON

I NEVER ALLOW myself to become discouraged under any circumstances. . . . The three great essentials to achieve anything worth while are, first, hard work; second, stick-to-itiveness; third, common sense.

CHARLES KINGSLEY

THANK GOD EVERY morning when you get up that you have something to do which must be done, whether you like it or not. Being forced to work, and forced to do your best, will breed in you temperance, self-control, diligence, strength of will, content, and a hundred other virtues which the idle never know.

HAROLD W. DODDS

NO, WORK IS not an ethical duty imposed upon us from without by a misguided and outmoded Puritan morality; it is a manifestation of man's deepest desire that the days of his life shall have significance.

from the writings of DALE CARNEGIE

I F YOU ARE devastated by sorrow, by disaster or calamity, get busy doing something. Keep your mind and your hands occupied. To do this will help you as nothing else will. I know. I have tried it.

⁓ FERENC MOLNÁR

"Work is the best narcotic!"

E XACTLY FIFTY YEARS ago my father gave me the words I have lived by ever since. He was a physician. I had just started to study law at the Budapest University. I failed one examination. I thought I could not survive the shame so I sought escape in the consolation of failure's closest friend, alcohol, always at hand: apricot brandy to be exact.

My father called on me unexpectedly. Like a good doctor he discovered both the trouble and the bottle in a second. I confessed why I had to escape reality.

The dear old man then and there improvised a prescription. He explained to me that there can be no real escape in alcohol or sleeping pills—or in any drug. For any sorrow there is only one medicine, better and more reliable than all the drugs in the world: work!

How right my father was! Getting used to work might be hard. Sooner or later you succeed. It has, of course, the quality of all the narcotics. It becomes habit-forming. And once the habit is formed, sooner or later, it becomes impossible to break one's self of it. I have never been able to break myself of the habit for fifty years.

◦§ JOHN RUSKIN

GOD INTENDS NO man to live in this world without working; but it seems to me no less evident that He intends every man to be happy in his work.

◦§ BENJAMIN FRANKLIN

DILIGENCE IS THE mother of good luck, and God gives all things to industry. Then plough deep while sluggards sleep, and you shall have corn to sell and to keep.

---

from the writings of DALE CARNEGIE

I'VE NEVER FELT sorry for anyone, man or woman, for having to earn a living. I do look with inestimable pity, however, on anyone who has no enthusiasm for the work he is doing. To me, it is a great tragedy if one does not find early in life the kind of work he likes to do that he may apply in full force all the enthusiasm of youth.

◦§ THE KORAN VIII

GOD HELPS THOSE who persevere.

◦§ WILLIAM SHAKESPEARE

Many strokes, though with a little axe,
Hew down and fell the hardest-timber'd oak.

————————— ◄(<(<(⊂)≻)≻)≻ —————————

from the writings of DALE CARNEGIE

THE PERSON WHO accepts responsibility makes himself stand out from the others in an office, a factory or in any walk in life, and he is the one who gets ahead. Welcome responsibility. Do this in little things and in big things, and success will come to you.

—————————————————————————————

WILLIAM SHAKESPEARE

AN ENTERPRISE, WHEN fairly once begun, should not be left till all that ought is won.

LOWELL THOMAS

DO A LITTLE more each day than you think you possibly can.

THOMAS A. EDISON

NEARLY EVERY MAN who develops an idea works it up to the point where it looks impossible, and then he gets discouraged. That's not the place to become discouraged.

HENRY WARD BEECHER

IN THE ORDINARY business of life, industry can do anything which genius can do, and very many things which it cannot.

from the writings of DALE CARNEGIE

To RAISE YOURSELF to a better position, you've got to do something special—make some extra effort. It won't be pleasant at the time, and it will mean hard grueling work while you're at it, but it will pay in the long run.

SIR JOSHUA REYNOLDS

EXCELLENCE IS NEVER granted to man but as the reward of labor. It argues no small strength of mind to persevere in habits of industry without the pleasure of perceiving those advances, which, like the hand of a clock, whilst they make hourly approaches to their point, yet proceed so slowly as to escape observation.

GEORGE ELIOT

IF WE WANT more roses, we must plant more trees!

JOHANN WOLFGANG VON GOETHE

THERE ARE BUT two roads that lead to an important goal and to the doing of great things: strength and perseverance. Strength is the lot but of a few privileged men; but austere perseverance, harsh and continuous, may be employed by the smallest of us and rarely fails of its purpose, for its silent power grows irresistibly greater with time.

━━━◦❨◦❨◦❨◻❩◦❩◦❩◦━━━

from the writings of DALE CARNEGIE

THERE ARE MANY things that go to make up success: good health (not always essential), energy—a producer of good health, perseverance, common sense, enthusiasm, talent. But one thing has been left out—the one thing without which all of the others together cannot produce success. That one thing: work!

⋗ELBERT HUBBARD

GENIUS IS ONLY the power of making continuous efforts. The line between failure and success is so fine that we scarcely know when we pass it: so fine that we are often on the line and do not know it. How many a man has thrown up his hands at a time when a little more effort, a little more patience, would have achieved success. As the tide goes clear out, so it comes clear in. In business sometimes, prospects may seem darkest when really they are on the turn. A little more persistence, a little more effort, and what seemed hopeless failure may turn to glorious success. There is no failure except in no longer trying. There is no defeat except from within, no really insurmountable barrier save our own inherent weakness of purpose.

⋗HENRY WADSWORTH LONGFELLOW

PERSEVERANCE IS A great element of success. If you only knock long enough and loud enough at the gate, you are sure to wake up somebody.

◄§CALVIN COOLIDGE

I HAVE FOUND it advisable not to give too much heed to what people say when I am trying to accomplish something of consequence. Invariably they proclaim it can't be done. I deem that the very best time to make the effort.

◄§CHARLES BUXTON

EXPERIENCE SHOWS THAT success is due less to ability than to zeal. The winner is he who gives himself to his work, body and soul.

---

from the writings of DALE CARNEGIE

YOU CAN GET ahead in the world. But you will have to work, you will have to want tremendously to accomplish something, and then be willing to pay the price. Are you willing?

◄§SIR ERNEST SHACKLETON

I NEVER UNDERTOOK anything of any measure in my life but what I was told that my effort would end in futility. This once caused me considerable worry. I no longer give it any heed.

from the writings of DALE CARNEGIE

MIX JUDGMENT WITH ambition and season it with energy. It makes a splendid recipe for success.

CALVIN COOLIDGE

NOTHING IN THE world can take the place of persistence. Talent will not; nothing is more common than unsuccessful men with talent. Genius will not; unrewarded genius is almost a proverb. Education will not; the world is full of educated derelicts. Persistence and determination alone are omnipotent. The slogan "Press on" has solved and always will solve the problems of the human race.

SIR THOMAS BUXTON

THE LONGER I live, the more I am certain that the great difference between men, between the feeble and the powerful, between the great and the insignificant, is energy—invincible determination —a purpose once fixed, and then death or victory. This quality will do anything that can be done in this world, and without it no circumstances, no talents, no opportunities will make a two-legged creature a man.

RUSSIAN PROVERB

PRAY TO GOD, but keep rowing to the shore.

HENRY FORD

IT HAS BEEN my observation that most people get ahead during the time that others waste.

ELBERT HUBBARD

FOLKS WHO NEVER do any more than they are paid for, never get paid for any more than they do.

---

from the writings of DALE CARNEGIE

MOST OF THE important things in the world have been accomplished by people who have kept on trying when there seemed to be no hope at all.

SAMUEL TAYLOR COLERIDGE

WHAT IS IT that first strikes us, and strikes us at once, in a man of education and which, among educated men, so instantly distinguishes the man of superior mind? . . . The true cause of the impression made upon us is that his mind is methodical.

THOMAS A. EDISON

GENIUS IS ONE per cent inspiration and ninety-nine per cent perspiration.

---

from the writings of DALE CARNEGIE

THE DIFFERENCE BETWEEN a successful person and a failure often lies in the fact that the successful man will profit by his mistakes and try again in a different way.

JOSEPH ADDISON

I NEVER KNEW an early-rising, hard-working, prudent man, careful of his earnings, and strictly honest, who complained of bad luck. A good character, good habits, and iron industry are impregnable to the assaults of all the ill luck that fools ever dreamed of.

BENJAMIN FRANKLIN

HE THAT RISETH late must trot all day, and shall scarce overtake his business at night; while laziness travels so slowly that poverty soon overtakes him. Drive thy business. Let it not drive thee.

ALEXANDER HAMILTON

MEN GIVE ME some credit for genius. All the genius I have lies in this: When I have a subject in hand, I study it profoundly. Day and night it is before me. I explore it in all its bearings. My mind becomes pervaded with it. Then the efforts that I make are what people are pleased to call the fruits of genius. It is the fruit of labor and thought.

⋙THOMAS CARLYLE

EVERY NOBLE WORK is at first impossible.

⋙HENRY WADSWORTH LONGFELLOW

The heights by great men reached and kept
Were not attained by sudden flight,
But they, while their companions slept,
Were toiling upward in the night.

from the writings of DALE CARNEGIE

IF YOU'VE BEEN unsuccessful in something you've wanted very much to do, don't give up and accept defeat. Try something else. You have more than one string for your bow—if only you will discover that string.

⋙SAMUEL JOHNSON

GREAT WORKS ARE performed, not by strength, but by perseverance. He that shall walk, with vigor, three hours a day will pass, in seven years, a space equal to the circumference of the globe.

—◄(‹(‹(:)›:)›:)›—

from the writings of DALE CARNEGIE

D ON'T LET ANYTHING discourage you. Keep on. Never
give up. That has been the policy of most of those
who have succeeded. Of course discouragement will
come. The important thing is to surmount it. If you can
do that, the world is yours!

ﻭWILLIAM SHAKESPEARE

SEE FIRST THAT the design is wise and just; that ascertained, pursue
it resolutely; do not for one repulse forgo the purpose that you
resolved to effect.

ﻭLLOYD GEORGE

TO TRUST TO the inspiration of the moment—that is the fatal phrase
upon which many promising careers have been wrecked. The surest
road to inspiration is preparation. I have seen many men of courage
and capacity fail for lack of industry. Mastery in speech can only
be reached by mastery in one's subject.

ﻭLORD NELSON

I OWE ALL my success in life to having been always a quarter of an
hour beforehand.

⊷SAMUEL JOHNSON

ALL THE PERFORMANCES of human art, at which we look with praise or wonder, are instances of the resistless force of perseverance: it is by this that the quarry becomes a pyramid, and that distant countries are united with canals. If a man was to compare the effect of a single stroke of the pickax or of one impression of the spade with the general design and last result he would be overwhelmed by the sense of their disproportion; yet those petty operations, incessantly continued, in time surmount the greatest difficulties, and mountains are leveled, and oceans bounded by the slender force of human beings.

5

Be true to yourself—be glad you're alive —be willing to learn! How much these three ideas have to offer in thinking about ourselves. We are *always* thinking about ourselves—there's nothing wrong with that —but let's do it constructively. ᏽ

CORNELIA OTIS SKINNER

PUBLIC OPINION WHICH, to be sure, can at times be helpful, must never for an instant swerve us from what we know in our hearts we *are* trying to convey. For honesty is the great requisite of art. If we remain honest with ourselves, art, which is always there, never lets us down.

ELEANOR ROOSEVELT

DO WHAT YOU feel in your heart to be right—for you'll be criticized anyway. You'll be damned if you do, and damned if you don't.

APOCRYPHA: ECCLESIASTICUS

LET THE COUNSEL of thine own heart stand; for there is no man more faithful unto thee than it. For a man's mind is sometime wont to tell him more than seven watchmen, that sit above in a high tower.

JOHN MILTON

GIVE ME THE liberty to know, to utter, and to argue freely according to conscience, above all liberties.

⋞WILLIAM SHAKESPEARE

And these few precepts in thy memory
See thou character. Give thy thoughts no tongue,
Nor any unproportion'd thought his act.
Be thou familiar, but by no means vulgar.
The friends thou hast, and their adoption tried,
Grapple them to thy soul with hoops of steel;
But do not dull thy palm with entertainment
Of each new-hatch'd, unfledg'd comrade. Beware
Of entrance to a quarrel; but being in,
Bear't that the opposed may beware of thee.
Give every man thine ear, but few thy voice;
Take each man's censure, but reserve thy judgment.
Costly thy habit as thy purse can buy,
But not express'd in fancy; rich, not gaudy;
For the apparel oft proclaims the man, . . .
Neither a borrower nor a lender be;
For loan oft loses both itself and friend,
And borrowing dulls the edge of husbandry.
This above all: to thine own self be true,
And it must follow, as the night the day,
Thou canst not then be false to any man.

⋞MARTIN F. TUPPER

KNOW THYSELF, THINE evil as well as thy good, and flattery shall
not harm thee; her speech shall be a warning, a humbling, and a
guide; for wherein thou lackest most, there chiefly will thy syco-
phant commend thee.

from the writings of DALE CARNEGIE

LET'S NOT WASTE a second worrying because we are not like other people. You are something new in this world. Never before, since the beginning of time, has there ever been anybody exactly like you; and never again throughout all the ages to come will there ever be anybody exactly like you again.

THOMAS H. HUXLEY

THERE IS NOTHING of permanent value (putting aside a few human affections), nothing that satisfies quiet reflection, except the sense of having worked according to one's capacity and light to make things clear and get rid of cant and shams of all sorts.

MARK TWAIN

IT WERE NOT best that we should all think alike; it is difference of opinion that makes horse races.

HENRY DAVID THOREAU

IF A PERSON lost would conclude that after all he is not lost, he is not beside himself, but standing in his own old shoes on the very spot where he is, and that for the time being he will live there; but the places that have known him, they are lost—how much anxiety and danger would vanish. I am not alone if I stand by myself. Who knows where in space this globe is rolling? Yet we will not give ourselves up for lost, let it go where it will.

———— ⋞⋘⋖⋘⋖(⋗⋗⋗⋗⋗⋗⋗⋗ ————

from the writings of DALE CARNEGIE

B
E YOURSELF. ACT on the sage advice that Irving Berlin gave the late George Gershwin. When Berlin and Gershwin first met, Berlin was famous but Gershwin was a struggling young composer working for thirty-five dollars a week in Tin Pan Alley. Berlin, impressed by Gershwin's ability, offered Gershwin a job as his musical secretary at almost three times the salary he was then getting. "But don't take the job," Berlin advised. "If you do, you may develop into a second-rate Berlin. But if you insist on being yourself, some day you'll become a first-rate Gershwin."

⊷⊷CONFUCIUS

VIRTUE CAN'T LIVE in solitude—neighbors are sure to grow up around.

⊷⊷RALPH WALDO EMERSON

I
T IS VERY easy in the world to live by the opinion of the world. It is very easy in solitude to be self-centered. But the finished man is he who in the midst of the crowd keeps with perfect sweetness the independence of solitude. I knew a man of simple habits and earnest character who never put out his hands nor opened his lips to court the public, and having survived several rotten reputations of younger men, Honor came at last and sat down with him upon his private bench from which he had never stirred.

————— ◄·(·<·(·<·(·❧·)·>·)·>·)·►= —————

from the writings of DALE CARNEGIE

IF HALF A century of living has taught me anything at all, it has taught me that "Nothing can bring you peace but yourself."

⊷MARCUS AURELIUS

HOW MUCH TIME he gains who does not look to see what his neighbor says or does or thinks.

⊷EDWIN MARKHAM

> Give me heart touch with all that live,
> And strength to speak my word;
> But if that is denied me, give
> The strength to live unheard.

⊷HENRY DAVID THOREAU

WHY SHOULD WE be in such haste to succeed and in such desperate enterprises? If a man does not keep pace with his companions, perhaps it is because he hears a different drummer. Let him step to the music which he hears, however measured or far away.

⊷THOMAS Á KEMPIS

GREAT TRANQUILITY OF heart is his who cares for neither praise nor blame.

✑MARK TWAIN

LIFE DOES NOT consist mainly—or even largely—of facts and happenings. It consists mainly of the storm of thoughts that is forever blowing through one's head.

✑RALPH WALDO EMERSON

TRUST THYSELF: EVERY heart vibrates to that iron string. Accept the place the divine providence has found for you, the society of your contemporaries, the connection of events. Great men have always done so, and confided themselves childlike to the genius of their age, betraying their perception that the absolutely trustworthy was seated at their heart, working through their hands, predominating in all their being. And we are now men, and must accept in the highest mind the same transcendent destiny; and not minors and invalids in a protected corner, not cowards fleeing before a revolution, but guides, redeemers, and benefactors, obeying the Almighty effort and advancing on Chaos and the Dark.

✑WILLIAM HAZLITT

HAPPY THOSE WHO live in the dream of their own existence, and see all things in the light of their own minds; who walk by faith and hope; to whom the guiding star of their youth still shines from afar, and into whom the spirit of the world has not entered!

✑CHARLES DE GAULLE

FACED WITH CRISIS, the man of character falls back on himself. He imposes his own stamp on action, takes responsibility for it, makes it his own. . . . Difficulty attracts the man of character because it is in embracing it that he realizes himself.

from the writings of DALE CARNEGIE

I HONESTLY BELIEVE that this is one of the greatest secrets to true peace of mind—a decent sense of values. And I believe we could annihilate fifty per cent of all our worries at once if we would develop a sort of private gold standard—a gold standard of what things are worth to us in terms of our lives.

MICHEL EYQUEM DE MONTAIGNE

"KNOW THYSELF" IS indeed a weighty admonition. But in this, as in any science, the difficulties are discovered only by those who set their hands to it. We must push against a door to find out whether it is bolted or not.

WALT WHITMAN

I celebrate myself, and sing myself,
And what I assume you shall assume
For every atom belonging to me as good belongs to you.

I loaf and invite my soul,
I lean and loaf at my ease observing a spear of summer grass.
My tongue, every atom of my blood, formed from this soil, this
      air,
Born here of parents born here from parents the same, and
      their parents the same,
I, now thirty-seven years old in perfect health, begin,
Hoping to cease not till death.

---

from the writings of DALE CARNEGIE

D ID YOU EVER see an unhappy horse? Did you ever see a bird that had the blues? One reason why birds and horses are not unhappy is because they are not trying to impress other birds and horses.

RALPH WALDO EMERSON

A FOOLISH CONSISTENCY is the hobgoblin of little minds, adored by little statesmen and philosophers and divines. With consistency a great soul has simply nothing to do. He may as well concern himself with his shadow on the wall. Speak what you think now in hard words, and tomorrow speak what tomorrow thinks in hard words again, though it contradict everything you said today. "Ah, so you shall be sure to be misunderstood." Is it so bad, then, to be misunderstood? Pythagoras was misunderstood, and Socrates, and Jesus, and Luther, and Copernicus, and Galileo, and Newton, and every pure and wise spirit that ever took flesh. To be great is to be misunderstood.

FRANÇOIS DE LA ROCHEFOUCAULD

THE CONFIDENCE WHICH we have in ourselves gives birth to much of that which we have in others.

ANNE MORROW LINDBERGH

THE MOST EXHAUSTING thing in life is being insincere.

⌐GEORGE BERNARD SHAW

YOU CAN NOT believe in honor until you have achieved it. Better keep yourself clean and bright; you are the window through which you must see the world.

⌐ABRAHAM LINCOLN

IF I WERE to try to read, much less to answer, all the attacks made on me, this shop might as well be closed for any other business. I do the very best I know how—the very best I can; and I mean to keep on doing so until the end. If the end brings me out all right, then what is said against me won't matter. If the end brings me out wrong, then ten angels swearing I was right would make no difference.

---

from the writings of DALE CARNEGIE

WE ALL HAVE possibilities we don't know about. We can do things we don't even dream we can do. It's only when necessity faces us that we rise to the occasion and actually do the things that hitherto have seemed impossible.

⌐HENRY CLAY

SIR, I WOULD rather be right than be President.

⌐DAVID STARR JORDAN

THE WORLD STANDS aside to let anyone pass who knows where he is going.

⇜§EDNA FERBER

ANY GARMENT WHICH is cut to fit you is much more becoming, even if it is not so splendid as a garment which has been cut to fit somebody not of your stature.

⇜§ABRAHAM LINCOLN

NO MAN HAS a good enough memory to be a successful liar.

⇜§DOUGLAS MALLOCH

If you can't be a pine on the top of the hill,
　　Be a scrub in the valley—but be
The best little scrub by the side of the hill;
　　Be a bush, if you can't be a tree.

If you can't be a bush, be a bit of the grass,
　　And some highway happier make;
If you can't be a muskie, then just be a bass—
　　But the liveliest bass in the lake.

We can't all be captains, we've got to be crew,
　　There's something for all of us here.
There's big work to do and there's lesser to do
　　And the task we must do is the near.

If you can't be a highway, then just be a trail,
　　If you can't be the sun, be a star;
It isn't by size that you win or you fail—
　　Be the best of whatever you are.

from the writings of DALE CARNEGIE

INSTEAD OF WORRYING about what people say of you, why not spend your time trying to accomplish something they will admire.

HELEN KELLER

NOW I AM as much up in arms against needless poverty and degrading influences as anyone else, but, at the same time, I believe human experience teaches that if we cannot succeed in our present position, we could not succeed in any other. Unless, like the lily, we can rise pure and strong above sordid surroundings, we would probably be moral weaklings in any situation. Unless we can help the world where we are, we could not help it if we were somewhere else. The most important question is not the sort of environment we have but the kind of thoughts we think every day, the kind of ideals we are following; in a word, the kind of men and women we really are. The Arab proverb is admirably true: "That is thy world wherein thou findest thyself."

LIN YUTANG

THE SECRET OF contentment is the discovery by every man of his own powers and limitations, finding satisfaction in a line of activity which he can do well, plus the wisdom to know that his place, no matter how important or successful he is, never counts very much in the universe. . . . The courage of being one's genuine self, of standing alone and of not wanting to be somebody else!

⇜§ABRAHAM LINCOLN

I DESIRE SO to conduct the affairs of this administration that if at the end, when I come to lay down the reins of power, I have lost every other friend on earth, I shall at least have one friend left, and that friend shall be down inside of me.

⇜§MARK TWAIN

ALWAYS DO RIGHT. This will gratify some people and astonish the rest.

⇜§WINSTON CHURCHILL

SO LONG AS I am acting from duty and conviction, I am indifferent to taunts and jeers. I think they will probably do me more good than harm.

⇜§HENRY DAVID THOREAU

DO WHAT YOU love. Know your own bone. Gnaw at it, bury it, unearth it, and gnaw it still.

⇜§HENRY FORD

ALL FORDS ARE exactly alike, but no two men are just alike. Every new life is a new thing under the sun; there has never been anything just like it before, and never will be again. A young man ought to get that idea about himself; he should look for the single spark of individuality that makes him different from other folks, and develop that for all he is worth. Society and schools may try to iron it out of him; their tendency is to put us all in the same mold, but I say don't let that spark be lost; it's your only real claim to importance.

from the writings of DALE CARNEGIE

THE THING FOR you to do is to find out which is the natural way for you to think. Then follow that method.

HARRY EMERSON FOSDICK

REBELLION AGAINST YOUR handicaps gets you nowhere. Self-pity gets you nowhere. One must have the adventurous daring to accept oneself as a bundle of possibilities and undertake the most interesting game in the world—making the most of one's best.

JOSHUA LOTH LIEBMAN

LET US . . . LEARN how to accept ourselves—accept the truth that we are capable in some directions and limited in others, that genius is rare, that mediocrity is the portion of almost all of us, but that all of us can contribute from the storehouse of our skills to the enrichment of our common life. Let us accept our emotional frailties, knowing that every person has some phobia lurking within his mind and that the normal person is he who is willing to accept life with its limitations and its opportunities joyfully and courageously.

ARTHUR SCHOPENHAUER

IT IS ONLY a man's own fundamental thoughts that have truth and life in them. For it is these that he really and completely understands. To read the thoughts of others is like taking the remains of someone else's meal, like putting on the discarded clothes of a stranger.

from the writings of DALE CARNEGIE

IF YOU CAN hold up your head and admit that you were in the wrong, then a wrong deed can benefit you. For to admit a wrong will not only increase the respect of those about you, it will increase your own self-respect.

CONFUCIUS

WHEN CONSCIENCE DISCOVERS nothing wrong, what is there to be uneasy about, what is there to fear?

RICHARD BURTON

Do what thy manhood bids thee do, from none but self expect
 applause;
He noblest lives and noblest dies who makes and keeps his self-
 made laws.

All other living is living death, a world where none but phantoms
 dwell,
A breath, a wind, a sound, a voice, a tinkling of the camel-bell.

THEODORE ROOSEVELT

WE HAVE GOT but one life here. . . . It pays, no matter what comes after it, to try and do things, to accomplish things in this life, and not merely to have a soft and pleasant time.

from the writings of DALE CARNEGIE

IF YOU WANT to be happy, set yourself a goal that commands your thoughts, liberates your energy and inspires your hopes. Happiness is within you. It comes from doing some certain thing into which you can put all your thought and energy. If you want to be happy, get enthusiastic about something outside yourself.

JOSEPH ADDISON

TRUE HAPPINESS IS of a retired nature and an enemy to pomp and noise; it arises, in the first place, from the enjoyment of one's self; and, in the next, from the friendship and conversation of a few select companions.

RALPH WALDO EMERSON

INSIST ON YOURSELF; never imitate. Your own gift you can present every moment with the cumulative force of a whole life's cultivation; but of the adopted talent of another, you have only an extemporaneous half-possession. That which each can do best none but his Maker can teach him.

WILLIAM LYON PHELPS

THE BELIEF THAT youth is the happiest time of life is founded on a fallacy. The happiest person is the person who thinks the most interesting thoughts, and we grow happier as we grow older.

&BENJAMIN FRANKLIN

Studious of ease, and fond of humble things,
Below the smiles, below the frowns of kings:
Thanks to my stars, I prize the sweets of life,
No sleepless nights I count, no days of strife.
I rest, I wake, I drink, I sometimes love,
I read, I write, I settle, or I rove;
Content to live, content to die unknown,
Lord of myself, accountable to none.

&NATHANIEL HAWTHORNE

INSINCERITY IN A man's own heart must make all his enjoyments, all that concerns him, unreal; so that his whole life must seem like a merely dramatic representation.

from the writings of DALE CARNEGIE

IF YOU HAVE some idea you believe in, don't listen to the croaking chorus. Listen only to what your own inner voice tells you.

&ABRAHAM LINCOLN

I BELIEVE THAT I shall never be old enough to speak without embarrassment when I have nothing to say.

&RALPH WALDO EMERSON

A MAN IS what he thinks about all day long.

⮑HENRY DAVID THOREAU

PUBLIC OPINION IS a weak tyrant, compared with our private opinion. What a man thinks of himself, that it is which determines, or rather indicates, his fate.

⮑DANIEL DEFOE

When the world trembles I'm unmoved;
When cloudy, I'm serene;
When darkness covers all without
I'm always bright within.

⮑MARCUS AURELIUS

IN THE MIND of him who is pure and good will be found neither corruption nor defilement nor any malignant taint. Unlike the actor who leaves the stage before his part is played, the life of such a man is complete whenever death may come. He is neither cowardly nor presuming; not enslaved to life nor indifferent to its duties; and in him is found nothing worthy of condemnation nor that which putteth to shame.

Test by a trial how excellent is the life of a good man—the man who rejoices at the portion given him in the universal lot and abides therein content; just in all his ways and kindly minded toward all men.

This is moral perfection; to live each day as though it were the last; to be tranquil, sincere, yet not indifferent to one's fate.

⮑HENRY VAN DYKE

BE GLAD OF life because it gives you the chance to love and to work and to play and to look up at the stars.

⇜ RICHARD E. BYRD

THE DAY WAS dying, the night being born—but with great peace. Here were the imponderable processes and forces of the cosmos, harmonious and soundless. Harmony, that was it! That was what came out of the silence—a gentle rhythm, the strain of a perfect chord, the music of the spheres, perhaps.

It was enough to catch that rhythm, momentarily to be myself a part of it. In that instant I could feel no doubt of man's oneness with the universe. The conviction came that that rhythm was too orderly, too harmonious, too perfect to be a product of blind chance —that, therefore, there must be purpose in the whole and that man was part of that whole and not an accidental offshoot. It was a feeling that transcended reason; that went to the heart of man's despair and found it groundless. The universe was a cosmos, not a chaos; man was as rightfully part of that cosmos as were the day and night.

⇜ HELEN KELLER

IT IS BEYOND a doubt that everyone should have time for some special delight, if only five minutes each day to seek out a lovely flower or cloud or a star, or learn a verse or brighten another's dull task. What is the use of such terrible diligence as many tire themselves out with, if they always postpone their exchange of smiles with Beauty and Joy to cling to irksome duties and relations? Unless they admit these fair, fresh, and eternal presences into their lives as they can, they must needs shut themselves out of heaven, and a gray dust settles on all existence. That the sky is brighter than the earth means little unless the earth itself is appreciated and enjoyed. Its beauty loved gives the right to aspire to the radiance of the sunrise and the stars.

HENRY JAMES

LIVE ALL YOU can; it's a mistake not to. It doesn't so much matter what you do in particular so long as you have your life. If you haven't had that, what have you had? I'm too old—too old at any rate for what I see. What one loses one loses; make no mistake about that. Still, we have the illusion of freedom; therefore, don't, like me today, be without the memory of that illusion. I was either, at the right time, too stupid or too intelligent to have it, and now I'm a case of reaction against the mistake. Do what you like so long as you don't make it. For it was a mistake. Live, live!

HENRY WADSWORTH LONGFELLOW

IF SPRING CAME but once in a century instead of once a year, or burst forth with the sound of an earthquake and not in silence, what wonder and expectation there would be in all hearts, to behold the miraculous change.

HENRY DAVID THOREAU

LOVE YOUR LIFE, as it is. You may perhaps have some pleasant, thrilling, glorious hours, even in a poorhouse. The setting sun is reflected as brightly from the windows of the almshouse as from the rich man's abode.

GEORGE BERNARD SHAW

I REJOICE IN life for its own sake. Life is no brief candle for me. It is sort of a splendid torch, which I have got hold of for the moment; and I want to make it burn as brightly as possible before handing it on to future generations.

from the writings of DALE CARNEGIE

IF YOU BELIEVE in what you are doing, then let nothing hold you up in your work. Much of the best work of the world has been done against seeming impossibilities. The thing is to get the work done.

✑ OLIVER WENDELL HOLMES

IT SEEMS TO me that life is like an artichoke. Each day, week, month, each year gives you one little bit which you nibble off—but there is precious little compared with what you throw away.

✑ THOMAS A. EDISON

IF WE ALL did the things we are capable of doing, we would literally astound ourselves.

✑ GEORGE BERNARD SHAW

THIS IS THE true joy in life, the being used for a purpose recognized by yourself as a mighty one; the being thoroughly worn out before you are thrown on the scrap heap; the being a force of Nature instead of a feverish selfish little clod of ailments and grievances complaining that the world will not devote itself to making you happy.

✑ BENJAMIN FRANKLIN

A LONG LIFE MAY not be good enough, but a good life is long enough.

≈§ WALT WHITMAN

Why, who makes much of a miracle?
As to me I know nothing else but miracles,
Whether I walk the streets of Manhattan,
Or dart my sight over the roofs of houses toward the sky,
Or wade with naked feet along the beach just in the edge of the
       water,
Or stand under trees in the woods,
Or talk by day with anyone I love, or sleep in the bed at night
      with anyone I love,
Or sit at table at dinner with the rest,
Or look at strangers opposite me riding in the car,
Or watch honeybees busy around the hive of a summer forenoon,
Or animals feeding in the fields,
Or birds, or the wonderfulness of insects in the air,
Or the wonderfulness of the sundown, or of stars shining so quiet
      and bright,
Or the exquisite delicate curve of the new moon in spring;
These with the rest, one and all, are to me miracles,
The whole referring, yet each distinct and in its place.

To me every hour of the night and dark is a miracle,
Every cubic inch of space is a miracle,
Every square yard of the surface of the earth is spread with the same,
Every foot of the interior swarms with the same.
To me the sea is a continual miracle,
The fishes that swim—the rocks—the motion of the waves—the ships
      with men in them,
What stranger miracles are there?

from the writings of DALE CARNEGIE

THE NEXT TIME you are tempted to run to someone else to get you out of some trouble, say to yourself, I can solve this problem myself. If I try to dodge, I am only fooling myself. I will solve it. Then go ahead and solve it. Then you have set your feet upon the path of success.

WILLIAM JAMES

COMPARED TO WHAT we ought to be, we are making use of only a small part of our physical and mental resources. Stating the thing broadly, the human individual thus lives far within his limits. He possesses powers of various sorts which he habitually fails to use.

HENRY DAVID THOREAU

OUR LIFE IS frittered away by detail. An honest man has hardly need to count more than his ten fingers, or in extreme cases he may add his ten toes, and lump the rest. Simplicity, simplicity, simplicity! I say, let your affairs be as two or three, and not a hundred or a thousand; instead of a million count half a dozen, and keep your accounts on your thumbnail. In the midst of this chopping sea of civilized life, such are the clouds and storms and quicksands and thousand-and-one items to be allowed for, that a man has to live, if he would not founder and go to the bottom and not make his port at all by dead reckoning, and he must be a great calculator who succeeds. Simplify, simplify. . . .

⇜MAURICE MAETERLINCK

TO LOOK FEARLESSLY upon life; to accept the laws of nature, not with meek resignation, but as her sons, who dare to search and question; to have peace and confidence within our souls—these are the beliefs that make for happiness.

⇜BENJAMIN DISRAELI

ACTION MAY NOT always bring happiness; but there is no happiness without action.

⇜WALT WHITMAN

The sun and stars that float in the open air;
The apple-shaped earth, and we upon it—
Surely the drift of them is something grand!
I do not know what is, except that it is grand, and that
Is happiness.

---

from the writings of DALE CARNEGIE

THAT IS WHAT every successful man loves: the game. The chance for self-expression. The chance to prove his worth, to excel, to win. That is what makes foot races and hog-calling and pie-eating contests. The desire to excel. The desire for a feeling of importance.

―――――=◁◁◁◁◁◁◁◁•◁(◁)•▷◁▷◁▷▷▷――――――

from the writings of DALE CARNEGIE

ACCORDING TO THE Book of Genesis, the Creator gave
man dominion over the whole wide earth. A mighty
big present. But I am not interested in any such super-
royal prerogatives. All I desire is dominion over myself
—dominion over my thoughts; dominion over my fears;
dominion over my mind and over my spirit. And the
wonderful thing is that I know that I can attain this
dominion to an astonishing degree, any time I want to,
by merely controlling my actions—which in turn control my reactions.

―――――――――――――――――――――――

≈ᵹANATOLE FRANCE

THE TRUTH IS that life is delicious, horrible, charming, frightful,
sweet, bitter, and that it is everything.

≈ᵹDAVID GRAYSON

JOY OF LIFE seems to me to arise from a sense of being where one
belongs. . . . All the discontented people I know are trying
sedulously to be something they are not, to do something they
cannot do. . . .

Contentment, and indeed usefulness, comes as the infallible
result of great acceptances, great humilities—of not trying to make
ourselves this or that (to conform to some dramatized version of
ourselves), but of surrendering ourselves to the fullness of life—
of letting life flow through us.

~&J. ROBERT OPPENHEIMER

ALL HISTORY TEACHES us that these questions that we think the pressing ones will be transmuted before they are answered, that they will be replaced by others, and that the very process of discovery will shatter the concepts that we today use to describe our puzzlement.

---

from the writings of DALE CARNEGIE

LET'S NOT GET so busy or live so fast that we can't listen to the music of the meadow or the symphony that glorifies the forest. Some things in the world are far more important than wealth; one of them is the ability to enjoy simple things.

~&HAROLD R. MEDINA

CAN A MAN truly be said to have this quality of wholeness or completeness unless he is filled with curiosity to seek out the truth, however it be veiled from his view and despite the difficulties which lie by the way?

~&JONATHAN EDWARDS

SURELY THERE IS something in the unruffled calm of nature that overawes our little anxieties and doubts: the sight of the deep-blue sky, and the clustering stars above, seems to impart a quiet to the mind.

———————◆◆◆◆◆◆◆◆◆——————————

from the writings of DALE CARNEGIE

STOP AND LOOK out the window and see how beautiful the world is. It is there—enjoy it. Go out tonight and and look up at the stars. They are the wonders of nature.

JEAN JACQUES ROUSSEAU

TO LIVE IS not merely to breathe, it is to act; it is to make use of our organs, senses, faculties, of all those parts of ourselves which give us the feeling of existence. The man who has lived longest is not the man who has counted most years, but he who has enjoyed life most. Such a one was buried a hundred years old, but he was dead from his birth. He would have gained by dying young; at least he would have lived till that time.

RALPH WALDO EMERSON

DO NOT BE too timid and squeamish about your actions. All life is an experiment. The more experiments you make the better. What if they are a little coarse, and you may get your coat soiled or torn? What if you do fail, and get fairly rolled in the dirt once or twice? Up again, you shall never be so afraid of a tumble.

ELEANOR ROOSEVELT

CHARACTER BUILDING BEGINS in our infancy and continues until our death.

✺§SIR ARTHUR HELPS

TO HEAR ALWAYS, to think always, to learn always, it is thus that we live truly; he who aspires to nothing, and learns nothing, is not worthy of living.

✺§GIUSEPPE MAZZINI

SLUMBER NOT IN the tents of your fathers. The world is advancing. Advance with it.

---

from the writings of DALE CARNEGIE

THE WORLD IS filled with interesting things to do. Don't lead a dull life in such a thrilling world.

✺§EMILY DICKINSON

We never know how high we are
Till we are called to rise;
And then, if we are true to plan,
Our statures touch the skies.

The heroism we recite
Would be a daily thing,
Did not ourselves the cubits warp
For fear to be a king.

━━━━━━━━ ◇❮◇❮◇❮❰◇❱◇❱◇❱◇❱◇ ━━━━━━━━

from the writings of DALE CARNEGIE

THIS IS THE only chance you will ever have on this earth with this exciting adventure called Life. So why not plan it, and try to live it as richly and as happily as possible?

❧ FRANK MOORE COLBY

EVERY MAN OUGHT to be inquisitive through every hour of his great adventure down to the day when he shall no longer cast a shadow in the sun. For if he dies without a question in his heart, what excuse is there for his continuance?

❧ RALPH WALDO EMERSON

NOW THAT IS the wisdom of man, in every instance of his labor, to hitch his wagon to a star, and see his chore done by the gods themselves.

❧ OLIVER WENDELL HOLMES

THE GREAT THING in this world is not so much where we are, but in what direction we are moving.

❧ THOMAS A. EDISON

THERE IS NO expedient to which a man will not resort to avoid the labor of thinking.

✍§WILLIAM JAMES

A GREAT MANY people think they are thinking when they are merely rearranging their prejudices.

✍§PLUTARCH

TO MAKE NO mistakes is not in the power of man; but from their errors and mistakes the wise and good learn wisdom for the future.

✍§THEODORE PARKER

EVERY MAN HAS, at times, in his mind the ideal of what he should be, but is not. In all men that seek to improve, it is better than the actual character. No one is so satisfied with himself that he never wishes to be wiser, better and more holy.

✍§HENRY DAVID THOREAU

MAN'S CAPACITIES HAVE never been measured; nor are we to judge of what he can do by any precedents, so little has been tried.

---

from the writings of DALE CARNEGIE

THE SMALL MAN flies into a rage over the slightest criticism, but the wise man is eager to learn from those who have censured him and reproved him and "disputed the passage with him."

————— ◄(◄(◄(◖)◄)◄)◄ —————

from the writings of DALE CARNEGIE

D^O YOU KNOW someone you would like to change and regulate and improve? Good! That is fine. I am all in favor of it. But why not begin on yourself? From a purely selfish standpoint, that is a lot more profitable than trying to improve others—yes, and a lot less dangerous.

"When a man's fight begins within himself," said Browning, "he is worth something." It will probably take from now until Christmas to perfect yourself. You can then have a nice long rest over the holidays and devote the new year to regulating and criticizing other people.

◖PHILLIPS BROOKS

BAD WILL BE the day for every man when he becomes absolutely contented with the life that he is living, with the thoughts that he is thinking, with the deeds that he is doing, when there is not forever beating at the doors of his soul some great desire to do something larger, which he knows that he was meant and made to do because he is still, in spite of all, the child of God.

◖ANONYMOUS

He that will not reason is a bigot,
He that cannot reason is a fool,
He that does not reason is a slave.

►§JOSEPH JOUBERT

THOSE WHO NEVER retract their opinions love themselves more than they love truth.

►§CHINESE PROVERB

WHO IS NOT satisfied with himself will grow; who is not sure of his own correctness will learn many things.

►§GEORGE A. DORSEY

THE MORE YOU use your brain, the more brain you will have to use.

---

from the writings of DALE CARNEGIE

KEEP YOUR MIND open to change all the time. Welcome it. Court it. It is only by examining and reexamining your opinions and ideas that you can progress.

►§ELBERT HUBBARD

THE RECIPE FOR perpetual ignorance is a very simple and effective one: be satisfied with your opinions and content with your knowledge.

►§THE TALMUD

BE EVER SOFT and pliable like a reed, not hard and unbending like a cedar.

✑§HELEN KELLER

FACE YOUR DEFICIENCIES and acknowledge them; but do not let them master you. Let them teach you patience, sweetness, insight. True education combines intellect, beauty, goodness, and the greatest of these is goodness. When we do the best that we can, we never know what miracle is wrought in our life, or in the life of another.

---

from the writings of DALE CARNEGIE

D O I PROFESS to know the answers to all those questions now? No. No man has ever been able to explain the mystery of life. We are surrounded by mysteries. The operation of your body is a profound mystery. So is the electricity in your home. So is the flower in the crannied wall. So is the green grass outside your window.

✑§BENJAMIN DISRAELI

A MAN CAN know nothing of mankind without knowing something of himself. Self-knowledge is the property of that man whose passions have their full play, but who ponders over their results.

✑§THOMAS CARLYLE

THE GREATEST OF faults, I should say, is to be conscious of none.

◆(⋅◈(⋅◈(⊏)❖⋅)❖⋅)❖

from the writings of D A L E   C A R N E G I E

WHEN I LOOK at the stars and realize that the light from some of these suns takes a million years to reach my eyes, I realize how tiny and insignificant this earth is, and how microscopic and evanescent are my own little troubles. I will pass on soon; but the sea stretching for a thousand miles in all directions and the stars and spiral nebulae swarming through illimitable space above, they will continue for thousands of millions of years. I marvel that any man looking up at the stars can have an exaggerated opinion of his own importance.

CPSIA information can be obtained
at www.ICGtesting.com
Printed in the USA
BVOW06s1930251117
501248BV00021B/1682/P